Women in Colonial India

Women in Colonial India

Essays on Politics, Medicine, and Historiography

Geraldine Forbes

CHRONICLE BOOKS
An Imprint of DC Publishers

New Delhi
2005

Chronicle Books is an imprint of DC Publishers

Distributed by
Orient Longman Limited

Bangalore Bhopal Bhubaneshwar Chandigarh
Chennai Ernakulam Guwahati Hyderabad Jaipur
Kolkata Lucknow Mumbai New Delhi Patna

ISBN 81-8028-017-9

Typeset in Bembo
by Eleven Arts, New Delhi
Printed in India by Pauls Press, New Delhi
Published by DC Publishers
D-27 NDSE Part II, New Delhi 110 049

Contents

For my granddaughter

Zoe Lee Greenblatt

Introduction

My interest in women's history began over three decades ago and within that time I have watched the discipline grow from a few studies to a robust field. In one of the first books on women in history, *Woman as Force in History* (1946), Mary Beard argued that women were history makers just like men but had been left out of the narrative. Beard resurrected women who played significant political roles and proved that, even when judged by the standards of male achievement, women had made history.[1] Almost three decades later, Gerda Lerner urged historians to make women's experiences their primary concern. Her pioneering work, *Women in American History* (1971), played a key role in developing a new feminist historiography.[2] Both historians were concerned with restoring women to history, Beard within the conventional parameters of history, and Lerner by reconceptualizing history to include women's lives.

In the United States, those writing women's history moved from discovery and celebration to re-examine the persistence of gender hierarchies, and more recently, to reconceptualize a wide range of topics using theoretical models from cultural studies. Some historians describe these as chronological "stages" in the development of the field but this hypothesis ignores the larger context. Throughout the world women's history has developed differently in different countries, and among groups within these countries, and cannot be separated from the political context.

My writing in women's history has not followed the American pattern for a number of reasons. First, I began writing women's history in the early 1970s without any formal training in what was then only emerging as a discipline. Second, I began writing about women not by design, but because I was given a remarkable and compelling document. From then on, I have moved from one research project to another, more because of sources I discovered than theoretical imperatives. Shudha Mazumdar, Manibehn Kara, Mithan Lam, Manmohini Zutshi Sahgal, and a number of other women gave me documents and talked to me for hours about their lives. The writings and ideas of these women have been extremely important in determining how I frame my questions. A central theme has dominated my research from the first exploration of *Positivism in Bengal* to my present work on family photographic collections. What fascinated me then and now is how people learn about, modify, and apply ideas and technology that come from outside their society.

I began with a memoir and have continued to work on women's writings about their own lives. Warned in the early 1970s that very few women had left records of their thoughts and activities, I am impressed with how much material we have recovered and preserved in the last three decades. Interested in the changes in women's lives brought by education, a later age of marriage, and new interests outside the home, I focused my attention on the late colonial period from the 1870s to the 1940s. The political demands of the Nationalist Movement had a profound effect on women, giving them new roles and opportunities to "prove" themselves in a very different milieu. At the same time, this movement redefined the "ideal Indian woman" and reinvigorated old ideas about motherhood and deference to male authority.

This collection includes essays in women's history written between 1979 and 2003, on politics, medicine, and historiography. My first published articles focused on the "new women" of the 1920s and 1930s who joined women's organizations and entered politics. When I look at some of these older articles, I see the impact of the times in which I wrote, especially the desire to celebrate women's achievements in difficult circumstances. I was also influenced by historians who urged us to look closely at the institutions that reproduced gender hierarchies and the extent to which women were complicit in these institutions. The three essays on politics in this volume illustrate these two influences. The first, "Caged Tigers: 'First Wave' Feminists in India," attempts to locate these individuals and this history within the larger context of world history. Although "feminism," because of its origins in the West and emphasis on individualism, is a problematic concept in India, I argue that the first women to enter political and social organizations were deeply concerned with improving women's status. The second of the political articles, "The Politics of Respectability: Indian Women and the Indian National Congress," examines how the parameters of women's entry into nationalist politics were set by male leaders and defined by women. The freedom struggle legitimized women's involvement in politics and presence outside the home but it did not liberate them from deeply held notions of female modesty and the necessity of male protection. The third article, "'Women of Character, Grit, and Courage;' The Reservation Debate in Historical Perspective," a rewrite of an earlier article on women's efforts to gain the vote, connects this movement to the current debate over reservations for women. Historically, activist women were trapped by their own rhetoric. While they used essentialist arguments to demand a role in politics, their connections to the Indian National Congress led them to support universal franchise. These two arguments were not compatible historically but, with universal franchise a fact of life in democratic India, many feminists now support reservations for women though for different reasons than their essentialist grandmothers.

My interest in colonial medicine began while reading the documents of the women's organizations that came to represent the voice of progressive Indian women. The members of these organizations defined themselves as modern, and although they were what others and I call "new women," they were also influenced and constrained by the reconfigured notion of the "ideal Indian woman." For example, they stood for equal educational opportunities but supported both separate schools for girls and home science education to make girls into efficient homemakers. At the same time, they insisted co-educational institutions be open to women who wanted to attend them. And, while they wanted to help poor women, they were seldom willing to work with prostitutes, and some worried they might be confused with their fallen sisters. In "Managing Midwifery in India," I look at their stand, solidly in favor of Western medical science and against indigenous traditions and *dhais*.

"Education to Earn: Training Women in the Medical Professions" is an attempt to compare medical education to non-professional education for women. In this essay, I have looked at three kinds of medical education for women—that for midwives, medical doctors, and hospital assistants—to answer questions about imperial motives, the role of Indian reformers, and the extent to which women were emancipated by schemes which provided professional training. In 1985, Joya Chaliha introduced me to Nomita De. Nomita's grandmother, Haimabati Sen, who left behind a memoir extraordinary for its frank discussion of the sexual and economic exploitation of women in late nineteenth and early twentieth century Bengal. Haimabati was one of India's early women doctors, but she had been trained as a "hospital assistant," not as a full-fledged doctor. In the final article in this section "Medicine for Women: 'Lady Doctors' in the Districts of Bengal," I explore the careers of Haimabati and her fellow graduates.

In recent years I have spent more time thinking about what we have accomplished (and left undone) in our efforts to write women's history. In "The First Step in Writing Women's History: Locating and Preserving Documents" I discuss a shared concern with the fragile material of women's history. At present there are many historians and archivists collecting and preserving women's documents but this was not always the case. Researchers who have engaged with this material for the last two decades are aware of what we have lost and how important it is to now look beyond written records and try to save photographs and women's memories. While I have been a tireless advocate for history which takes note of gender, I turn to my concerns about the insularity of the field in the final essay in this collection, "Reflections on South Asian

Women's History." In the early days, we argued for a separate women's history because the history being written overlooked women and ignored gender as a category of analysis. Our goal was a new history, a new metanarrative inclusive of women and gender. Increasingly, young historians have lost sight of this goal to pursue topics that are funny and interesting, but intrinsically apolitical. In "Reflections," I argue that we cannot afford to ignore the impact of international politics and globalization on ourselves as historians and on the histories we write.

ACKNOWLEDGMENTS

In the three decades that I have been researching women's lives, I have been encouraged, prodded, and assisted by mentors, colleagues, friends, and research assistants. Blair Kling, my advisor at the University of Illinois, Urbana-Champaign, tolerated my seminar papers on child marriage and other social issues, and with Edward C. Dimock, encouraged my first work in women's history. In India, Tarun Mitra, former director of the American Institute of Indian Studies in Calcutta, has for the length of my time in India guided me to valuable sources, made suggestions, and offered advice. Research assistants, the late Tridib Ghosh, Jayati Chaliha, Mandira Bhaduri, Haimanti Roy, and Satarupa Bose Roy have done invaluable work searching out records and documents, translating, making suggestions, and commenting on my papers. Archivists Richard Bingle, Rosemary Seton, and Abhijit Bhattacharya have done more than I could have ever wished to make my research go smoothly.

Among my colleagues in the USA and England, I would like to thank Mrinalini Sinha, Antoinette Burton, Sylvia Vatuk, Rosy Fitzgerald, Veena Oldenburg, Swapna Banerjee, Susan Wadley, and Padma Anagol for their generous and continuing support. Barbara Ramusack deserves special mention for her generous mentoring for almost three decades. And, I would be remiss if I did not mention my colleagues in Women's Studies and History at The State University of New York, Oswego for listening to early versions of these ideas and papers. In India and Bangladesh, C.S. Lakshmi, Joya Chaliha,

Rana and Ben Behal, Neera Desai, Usha Thakkar, Sonia Nishat Amin, Paula Banerjee, Tanika Sarkar, Anuradha Chanda, Maitreyi Krishnaraj, Vina Mazumdar, Jasodhara Bagchi, Janaki Nair, and the late Ranjit Roy, have been of immeasurable help with their suggestions and comments.

Over the years I have received scholarships and research fellowships from my own institution, The State University of New York, and from the American Institute of Indian Studies, the Ford Foundation, the Smithsonian Institution, the National Endowment for the Humanities, and the Fulbright Foundation. Without these grants I could not have traveled so often to India and the U.K. for research and conferences.

My husband Sidney Greenblatt, my stepson, David Greenblatt, and daughter-in-law, Saejung Lee, share my passion for India and for social justice. They have been in India with me and met some of the women I write about. Without their love and support, research would be far less fun.

Included in this volume are revisions of the following essays:

"Caged Tigers: 'First Wave' Feminists in India," from *Women's Studies International Forum,* 5: 6 (1982), pp. 525–536, with permission from Elsevier.

"The Politics of Respectability: Indian Women and the INC," from *The Indian National Congress,* ed. Anthony Low (Delhi: Oxford University Press, 1988:), pp. 54–97, with permission from Oxford University Press India.

"'Women of Character, Grit, and Courage:' The Reservation Debate in Historical Perspective," from *Between Tradition, Counter Tradition and Heresy: Contributions in Honour of Vina Mazumdar,* ed. Kumud Sharma (New Delhi: Rainbow Publishers, 2002), pp. 221–39, with permission from The Centre for Women's Development Studies, Delhi.

"Managing Midwifery in India," from *Contesting Colonial Hegemony: State and Society in Africa and India,* eds. Dagmar Engels and Shula Marks (London: British Academic Press, an imprint of I.B. Tauris, 1994), pp. 152–72, with permission from I.B. Tauris.

"Medicine for Indian Women: Campbell Medical School Graduates in the Districts of Bengal," presented at the Conference on South Asia, Madison, WI. (October, 1996) in a panel on "The Modernization of Health Care in India: Women as Practitioners and Patients."

"Colonial Imperatives and Women's Emancipation: Western Medical Education for Indian Women in Nineteenth Century Bengal," from *Modern Historical Studies*, 2 (2001), pp. 83–102, with permission from Rabindra Bharati University.

"Locating and Preserving Documents: The First Step in Writing Women's History," from the *Journal of Women's History*. Special Issue Revising *the Experiences of Colonized Women: Beyond Binaries*. (Winter, 2003), pp. 169–78, with permission from Indiana University Press.

"Reflections on South Asian Women's/Gender History: Past and Future," from the *Journal of Colonialism and Colonial History* 4:1 (2003) with permission from The Johns Hopkins University Press.

Politics

Caged Tigers
"First Wave" Feminists in India

"No feminist works emerged from behind the Hindu purdah[1] or out of the Moslem harems; centuries of slavery do not provide a fertile soil for intellectual development or expression." So wrote Miriam Schneir in her introduction to a book entitled *Feminism: the Essential Historical Writings.*[2] In this short statement, Schneir justified the publication of a collection of articles solely by Western women, and denied Indian (and other Asian and Middle Eastern) women their feminist heritage. But Schneir was wrong on a number of counts. If we agree on a definition of feminism as a set of doctrines "on the place of women in society, and . . . on the extent to which women should have equal rights, opportunities and responsibilities with those of men,"[3] then feminism existed in India. Indian women wrote and spoke about women's condition, formed organizations to secure desired change, and eventually had an impact on the institutions of their society. Moreover, like their Western sisters, their concerns during the first phase of feminism (the 1880s to the 1940s) were the political and legal superstructure.[4] And, their most notable reforms were in the areas of suffrage, education, and legal and civil rights. But, they were not carbon copies of Western feminists in either ideology or goals. India was under British rule, its economy was subordinated to British needs, and the Indian social system bore little resemblance to that of Western nations. Despite these differences, feminism did emerge from behind the purdah.

The nineteenth century witnessed the consolidation of British power in India and the acceleration of Western contact which brought far-reaching changes in the social structure. Detailed studies of women's status do not exist for the early nineteenth century but the information available suggests that political disruption further eroded their status. Ideally, traditional law and custom struck a balance between the protection of women (who were considered dependent throughout their lives) and respect for women. Women might have power and authority, but not autonomy.[5] Protecting women had become the major concern of the elite and this resulted in arranged marriages for young girls, no remarriage for virgin widows, encouraging sati or immolation on the husband's funeral pyre as an act of devotion, prohibitions on female education, and rigid enforcement of the rules of seclusion. Legally, women were denied the same rights as men in matters of inheritance, property ownership, and the guardianship of children.

Customs which denied women access to education and their humanity came under attack by the Indian intelligentsia at the beginning of the nineteenth century. Influenced by Western ideas and by a Renaissance which involved a rediscovery of their own traditions, a number of reformers began to champion the cause of women. Rammohun Roy, often called the "Father of Modern India," attacked the notion that women were morally inferior. In a tract denouncing sati, Rammohun declared women morally superior to men but unable to demonstrate their capabilities because they were denied education.[6] While some reformers appealed to the "Golden Age" of Hinduism (the Vedic Age, c. 1500–500 BC) for proof that contemporary customs did not have ancient sanction, others critiqued their society in terms that would be acceptable to contemporary feminism. Vidyasagar, a famous Sanskritist and educationalist of the nineteenth century, emerged as a champion of widow-remarriage and female education. In the preface to his first tract on the evils of polygamy (1871) he explained why women submitted to and participated in degrading customs:

Women are comparatively weak and due to the tyranny of social custom subordinated to men. Owing to this weakness and domination by men, women have to spend their lives in ignominy and subordination. The dominant male tyrannize over, and exploit them according as they like, and women have helplessly to submit to the same and eke out their existence.[7]

Both groups of reformers, revivalists and progressives, shared a concern with the status of women and were instrumental in beginning a movement directed towards changing the reality of their times.

Efforts to provide education for Indian females had begun early in the nineteenth century, but these efforts met with little success until the idea of female education had gained respectability amongst the intelligentsia. Foreign missionaries were instrumental in educating the daughters of Christian converts who later became teachers in the schools sponsored by reformist Hindus and Muslims. It was not until the middle of the nineteenth century that these reformist groups began to sponsor schools which reflected a new evaluation of females and the perception of an enlarged female role.

Soon after, these same reform groups sponsored the earliest formal organization for women. Umesh Chandra Dutt, a member of the Brahmo Samaj, founded both a women's organization and a women's journal. The organization was to give women a place to meet and discuss their problems; the journal would provide an outlet for their literary efforts as well as reading material for the growing body of literate females.[8] While the efforts of the Brahmos of Bengal resulted in the earliest organizations for women, similar reform groups organized women's associations in other parts of India.

As women became literate and found a "voice," they were able to express their own version of women's positions, grievances, and solutions. The early works of these women manifest a deep concern with "tearing the purdah," "breaking out of the cage," and "escaping from bondage." Imposed seclusion kept them from education and from knowing about and experiencing the world outside the home and family. Although a number of these early writers were concerned with female education and a few thought females should have some say in the choice of marriage partners, the main target was the purdah system. They saw these elaborate rules about women's proper place as the major cause of their subordinate status. They complained about the many ways women were kept in bondage and argued they should be given greater freedom. But since most of these writers were still living restricted lives, they offered no coherent vision of what they would accomplish as emancipated women.[9] They were not feminists in the sense of an Elizabeth Cady Stanton[10] who spoke about what women would achieve once free to act as citizens, rather they were crying out against customs that kept them in chains.

Despite their protests against the harsh aspects of seclusion, few of these women were ready to abandon sex-segregation. The earliest associations of women were "ladies' gatherings" attached to larger social reform organizations. Examples of women speaking in public or even attending mixed gatherings were rare. Women first met in local associations, organized by male reformers on their behalf; later they attended the ladies' gatherings of all-Indian reform associations. An early example of this type of ladies auxiliary was the Bharata Mahila Parishad [Indian Women's Conference], inaugurated in 1904 as part of the National Social Conference begun in 1887. Newspaper reports called this the largest gathering of women Bombay had ever seen. The meeting had been arranged solely by women who decided no men would be allowed to enter the hall. Ramabai Ranade, the widow of the well-known reformer Justice M.G. Ranade, urged women to work together for the regeneration of the nation.[11] Other speakers focused on the need for female education and discussed social issues such as lack of medical care, early marriage, and child welfare.[12] In subsequent meetings, held yearly in conjunction with the meetings of the National Social Conference, between 300 and 700 women attended. They discussed women's problems and what women could do to change the situation. Education was foremost on their list, followed by child marriage and the problems of widows and dowry. They were just beginning to formulate strategies for women; most of their efforts were still directed towards understanding and formulating issues.[13]

With experience, the women attending these meetings began to see the need for organizations of their own. It was through these women's organizations, formed between 1910 and 1927, that a demand for women's rights was articulated and tactics developed for affecting the power structure. The attempt of Maharashtrian women to form their own association (to honor Justice Ranade) was opposed by a group of males who preferred a joint organization.

One of the women involved explained why women wanted to meet without men:

Public spirited women are for the present in a minority and their individual efforts and eloquence would be submerged by the superior and voluminous activities of men, if a combination took place. The minority of their number and the newness of their experiences may prevent their influence from asserting itself in any movement in which they were joined by men . . . [14]

Moreover, men might not want to concede women their rights.

Saraladevi Chaudhurani, a well-educated woman and radical nationalist, used the Ladies Conference of the National Social Conference to propose the formation of a women-only organization: Bharat Stree Mahamandal [The Great Circle of Indian Women]. She too was opposed by male reformers who thought separate meetings unnecessary. Saraladevi chided these men with "pretending" to be champions of women when they actually wanted to supervise their discussions and control their actions. Saraladevi had been inspired by what she knew about the YWCA and hoped that the Mahamandal would develop a "sisterhood" that could supply an endless number of energetic Indian women ready to work to improve the condition of women. At the first meeting of the Mahamandal, in Allahabad in 1910, the members decided to concentrate on educating women who lived under purdah. Emulating the missionaries, the Mahamandal offered zenana education, that is, lessons within the home which upheld the norms of female modesty. The Mahamandal, and particularly women like Saraladevi, opposed the seclusion of women but believed zenana education and neighborhood schools could fight the crippling features of this custom.[15] Sex-segregation was seen as both harmful and beneficial. On the one hand, it deprived women of education and knowledge of the world; on the other hand, it gave adequate justification for women's own organizations and the articulation of women's problems. The Mahamandal developed a number of branches offering zenana education, which proved extremely expensive. Within a few years only two or three branches survived.

A far more durable organization was the Women's Indian Association [WIA] begun in Madras in 1917 by merging the Tamil Women's Association (a branch of the Mahamandal) with a women's improvement society begun by two foreign women, Dorothy Graham Jinarajadasa and Margaret Cousins. Both Jinarajadasa and Cousins were converts to Theosophy then under the leadership of the famed feminist and birth control advocate, Annie Besant. All three of these women had been connected with militant feminism in the British Isles. While their tactics had softened following their conversion to theosophy and move to India, they were still deeply concerned with the improvement of women's status.

Using the networks of the Theosophical Lodges, Jinarajadasa set about building branches of the Women's Indian Association. India's future rests with its women, she had written to lodge inspectors and secretaries, and women must come together to work out ways to improve their position.[16] The aim of the new organization, according to one of its founder-members, Kamalabai L. Rau, was to educate women and make them "conscious of their place in the growing society of the land."[17] Organizing meetings was not easy, but in each region there were a few women who had already been touched by the changes taking place and they worked diligently to bring women together, arrange reading classes and lectures, and encourage discussion of social issues. From this small beginning, local organizations began to discuss and pass resolutions on topics such as votes for women, the prevention of child marriage, and inheritance rights for women. These demands were then presented to the appropriate officials in the government.[18] The first women's delegation to demand the vote included a large number of WIA members and in the following years it was this organization which took the lead in mobilizing support for female franchise.[19]

The National Council of Women in India [NCWI] was formally founded in 1925 when it was accepted as the national "branch" of the International Council of Women. It thus became the first all-India women's organization intimately associated with an international body. While this inhibited its development in a period of growing nationalism, it provided an opportunity to voice Indian opinion at international forums. Growing out of the Bombay Council organized for war work, the NCWI sought to affiliate various groups, act as a voice for its affiliates and as a clearing house for various kinds of work being done to help women. Supported by British women and many of India's titled and wealthy women, the Council lacked the nationalist fervor found in other women's organizations. Nevertheless, this did not prevent it from sharing a feminist ideology and at times, acting very effectively to express women's issues in the political arena.

The most important women's organization formed in this period was the All India Women's Conference [AIWC] which first met in January of 1927. Originally the organizers had no intention of forming another women's association, they were a group of activist women who met to discuss female education and present their demands to the government. Margaret Cousins, organizer of the first meeting, was responding to a challenge that had been publicly voiced by the Director of Public Instruction in Bengal. Presiding over a prize-giving ceremony at a women's college in Calcutta, the director called upon Indian women to tell the government "with one voice" what kind of education they wanted. The principal of the college wrote an article on his speech for the WIA organ, *Stri Dharma*, and Margaret Cousins followed up with letters to the WIA branches. First local conferences were held, then delegates met in Poona to discuss the larger issues. The delegates included a number of well-educated women with careers in education and social work. These women had personally moved far from the secluded environment yet they worked with women still secluded. When they discussed education, they realized it was difficult to separate this issue from social customs which kept females away from school. Purdah and child marriage could not be ignored, they argued. When the Conference was formed the founders recognized they would have to talk about social as well as educational issues. Before long it became obvious that these topics could not be separated from politics and the AIWC, along with other organizations, began to consider Indian nationalism as well as "women's issues."

These women rejected the English label "feminist" because it implied that they put women's rights before those of the nation and viewed men as the enemy. They defined their enemy as "custom," which they saw as the result of wars, invasions, and imperialism. Their concerns were "women's issues," many of which had their origins in the nineteenth century reform movement, but these could not be separated from a concern with freedom from foreign dominance and exploitation. Their ideology of women's rights gained its legitimacy from the notion of the "Golden Age" when women were free to participate in political and social affairs. They promoted an enlarged role for women who could bring their special "womanly" talents to improve the world.

Sarojini Naidu (1879–1949), an extraordinary woman and forceful leader whose career encompassed both the women's movement and the political movement, was one of many who spoke and wrote on these themes. "New women," she declared, were in touch with their roots and the spiritual descendants of the heroines of ancient epics. However, they needed to move outside the home and family and act like epic heroines in the larger arena of the nation.[20] The home had always been the essential institution of Indian civilization, and within that home, "the mother is the immemorial keeper of that tradition that means purity, honour, love, service, and sacrifice for the glory of the nation."[21] In her speech as President of the Indian National Congress, Sarojini developed a model with India as the "house," the Indian people as "members of the joint family," and the Indian woman as "Mother." Women had to use their talents to put the national "house" in order, reconcile the tragic quarrels between joint family members, and find a place in the "home" for all the children and foster-children.[22] Her notion of the role that women would play in the new India incorporated a denunciation of customs which prevented women from playing that role: child marriage, seclusion, and prohibitions against female education. Sarojini's generation had advanced far beyond the first women who cried out against seclusion. For the women of the 1920s and 1930s it was clear that freedom from restrictive customs would make it possible for them to contribute to the regeneration of India.

Sarojini Naidu, 1919
(Nehru Memorial
Museum and Library)

Sarojini Naidu and other women leaders worked to secure the vote for women, destroy social customs they saw as detrimental to women's equal development, encourage female education, and change the legal framework which affected women's lives. At the same time, a struggle against British dominance was being waged by constitutionalists, Gandhians, and violent revolutionaries. All three groups saw the value of having women in their movements and denounced Western feminism as pitting women against men. And, women joined each of these groups. It was in dealing with specific issues that the question of women's rights versus nationalism proved difficult. A number of women's issues—education for females, the right to vote, legislation to protect women in mines and factories, employment for women, and the amelioration of the condition of widows—posed no problem by the 1920s. However, other concerns such as child marriage, legislation affecting property and the family, and purdah were potentially divisive.

Most modernists, male and female, opposed child marriage. However, some nationalists and many Muslim and Hindu conservatives resisted government interference in religious matters. Marriage law, which included age of marriage, remained under the authority of the religious texts of each specific religion. From their inception, both the WIA and the AIWC had recognized child marriage as a detriment to female education and health.[23] As soon as the Hindu Child Marriage Bill was introduced in 1927, these organizations mobilized to lend it their support. Following study and amendment, the Child Marriage Restraint Act, which applied to members of all religious communities, was passed in 1929. Because the AIWC had been particularly active in holding meetings, presenting petitions, sending delegations to meet members of the Legislative Assembly, writing articles, and presenting evidence, they regarded this as their "personal triumph."[24] The Child Marriage Restraint Act actually helped to solidify the connection between the women's movement and the nationalist movement. Women believed they had removed one of the main stumbling blocks to female education and the result would be the fuller participation of women in the political and social life of the emerging nation. Indian nationalists had assured these women's groups they would support their reformist agenda. However, the years immediately following the passage of this act taught all concerned that they ought not to have been so optimistic about the efficacy of legislation.[25]

Purdah was more problematic. Seclusion inside a house, no matter how large and luxurious, had caused women to liken their condition to that of birds in a cage. However, many other women observed purdah yet traveled about to attend meetings and make speeches. These women, who made ample use of closed carriages, women's compartments, and the burqa,[26] saw observance of purdah as a conscious choice made for religious and/or social reasons. One woman related that she observed purdah when she did not want to meet her husband's guests.[27] It would seem that these women wanted both mobility and choice; demands to abolish veiling or force co-education were rarely heard. The members of the Indian women's organizations attacked purdah as inhibiting female education yet they worked for separate schools for girls, set up Lady Irwin College, a home science college for women, demanded women's hospitals, and asked for separate women's compartments on trains and buses. Moreover, they urged the government to provide schools for girls where strict purdah could be maintained (by sending covered carriages to pick up the girls, providing covered entrances, surrounding the school with high walls, and vigorously excluding males from the grounds), to provide purdah hospitals, and to set up purdah parks. They did not condone purdah, nor did they think it could be easily abolished.

Despite this accommodation to purdah, it became an issue that divided Hindu women from Muslim women. Both religions mandated that women be modest and under the guardianship of men, and women of both religions observed purdah. However, modernist Hindus and Muslims denied that rigid purdah derived from their respective religions. Hindus spoke of the "Golden Age" when women moved freely and Muslims argued that during Muhammad's time ordinary women were not veiled or restricted in their movements. The abuses of the system were regarded as the result of "custom," further explained by some as an imitation of Muslim or Hindu court customs, or as practices adopted to protect women during the Muslim invasions. Muthulaksmi Reddi blamed patriarchal society and male attitudes towards women. Reddi, a practicing doctor and ardent women's rights advocate, saw purdah as an outmoded custom, deriving from the days of constant warfare. It continued into modern times because men felt superior to women, regarded them as temptresses, and failed to recognize they had intelligence.[28] But her analysis of purdah was never popularized. Instead, Hindu feminists began to see purdah as a custom brought to India by Muslim invaders and a cause of women's fall from the high position they held during the "Golden Age."[29] As the nationalist movement intensified, so did antagonism between India's two major religions. Fearing they would be swamped in a free India ruled by the Hindu majority, the Muslim minority became increasingly concerned with their identity as Muslims. Muslim feminists admitted the Quran contained passages about female modesty, but denied that Indian-style purdah could be blamed on Islam. What had been the feminist issue of the nineteenth century had, by the third decade of the twentieth century, become an issue which divided Hindu feminists, with their insistence on a particular interpretation of the "Golden Age," from Muslim feminists, who had grown protective of their religion. While discussion of purdah caused a rift between advocates of women's rights, the custom itself was never vigorously attacked.

Reform of women's legal status, particularly in relation to family law, became a major issue for women's organizations and caused a split between nationalists and feminists. From their inception, women's organizations had discussed women's legal status. The Women's Indian Association began by requesting the vote for women. The All-India Women's Conference plunged into support for the Child Marriage Restraint Act, and the National Council concerned itself with issues discussed in the League of Nations and other international bodies. One issue quite naturally led to another and by the 1930s, women's right to divorce and to inherit and control property emerged as salient issues.[30] Throughout the 1930s women's organizations formed legal committees, undertook studies of the laws, consulted with lawyers, published pamphlets on women's legal status, and encouraged legislation designed to improve women's position. By 1934, the AIWC had passed a resolution demanding a Hindu Code that would modify the laws governing marriage and inheritance. In requesting these changes, they were supported by reformist members of the Legislative Assembly who believed law was a legitimate method of social change. In 1933, V.V. Joshi, a High Court pleader from Baroda, wrote a pamphlet for distribution by the AIWC. In this pamphlet he supported the appointment of a government committee to inquire into women's legal disabilities and suggest reform. Such a committee was finally appointed in 1941 but by this time the Indian National Congress was boycotting the legislatures and a number of Congress leaders had already gone to jail. Within a few months, thousands of Congress members were engaged in Civil Disobedience. Cooperating with this government-appointed committee could be construed as opposition to Congress and Gandhi, who insisted women's true liberation was intimately tied to the liberation of India. For those women who decided to put nationalism first, the decision to boycott the committee was not difficult. However, there were many women who had not made this choice. At the sixteenth annual conference of the AIWC (1941–1942), Vilasini Devi Shenai argued against putting nationalism first:

Today our men are clamouring for political rights at the hands of an alien government. Have they conceded their wives, their own sisters, their daughters, "flesh of their flesh, blood of their blood" social equality and economic justice?[31]

Her arguments and those of other like-minded women won the day in this organization. In January 1944, the AIWC supported the reconstitution of the Rau Committee, to prepare a Hindu Code.[32] Despite the organization's decision, a number of members stood with Congress on this issue. In the final analysis, the Hindu Code did not become law until after Indian Independence in 1947. Between 1955 and 1956 the Code passed piecemeal through parliament, owing as much to the perseverance of Prime Minister Jawaharlal Nehru as to the lobbying efforts of the women's organizations. The decision of women's rights advocates to support the committee's efforts in 1944 had not caused Congress to abandon social reform.

CONCLUSIONS

First wave feminism gradually subsided following Independence. The Indian Constitution promised women complete equality. The new legal codes abolished social restrictions, and the new bureaucratic structure included institutions designed to improve women's status. Many have credited these gains to women's participation in the nationalist movement, arguing these were their "rewards" for marching, demonstrating, and picketing on behalf of nationalist objectives. A more careful reading of the documents make it clear that male leaders were not united in support of women's rights. Some of the most important leaders, for example Mahatma Gandhi and Jawaharlal Nehru, were committed to improving women's position. Others disagreed that social legislation and civil rights were the appropriate means for attaining this aim. However, they understood that women wanted rights and would organize to obtain them. Women's willingness to fight for political and legal rights, often in defiance of male authority, is one of the significant accomplishments of first-wave feminism.

The women who accomplished these reforms were affiliated with the major women's organizations and, in some cases, with nationalist parties. The women's organizations—WIA, AIWC, and NCWI—were all "pro-India" but differed in terms of the degree to which they were "anti-British." All three organizations agreed, however, that India would be better off making its own laws. Women were expressing great faith in the reformist attitudes of their fellow-countrymen.

Although these women were concerned with legislation, they aimed at social change and understood that it would not come easily or quickly. Their writings and statements make it clear that their long range goal was equality. Writing about the newly proposed legislation and the discussions taking place, Sarojini Naidu noted:

The supreme overlordship of man and particularly that of the husband is strongly questioned. The women seek to have their own free choice in the selection of partners in life, the right to enter the state of Motherhood when and if they desire, to seek divorce if necessity arises. These are some of the problems upon which the movement is working.[33]

When Nehru critiqued the women's organizations for being "superficial" in their analysis of women's problems, Kamaladevi Chattopadhyay, a socialist, nationalist, and leader of the women's movement, suggested he be more charitable. She doubted he truly understood the social prejudice women encountered in their lives and the world they were trying to change. The fight against the rigid codes of society was more difficult and less glamorous than any political struggle, Kamaladevi maintained.[34] Some women, it is true, expressed satisfaction with the legislative victories, but many more continued to work with associations designed to ameliorate the sufferings of those women who were victims of an unjust system. Only a few women continued to imagine complete equality.

This period deserves our attention because it has been so misunderstood. Observers of the contemporary Indian scene tend either to see the women's movement as part and parcel of the movement to gain political independence, to disregard it as a parody of Western feminism, or to evaluate it in terms of the present condition of Indian women. Many of the women who were concerned with women's rights were part of the political movement, but almost all of them had come to "politics" through "social work." Helena Dutt, a member of one of the revolutionary parties in Bengal, described herself and her friends as extremely eager to take advantage of neighborhood schools being set up in the 1920s. They were "thirsty" for education, she recalled, "Bengali girls were like caged tigers—once the gate was opened, they leapt out." When these newly educated young women began doing "social work," they became conscious of the inequality of the system and the hardships of women. As their consciousness of the world and women's place in it grew, they began to understand the role of political power in shaping that world.[35] For many, improving the position of women and freeing India from British rule were intertwined. India could not make its own laws and the British had demonstrated their lack of interest in social legislation. Women's rights seemed dependent on freedom from imperialism. If they fought for freedom first, it was not because they were willing to put women's issues aside. Rather, they saw themselves as working for women's rights when they demonstrated, marched or supported revolutionary activities.

That Indian women were unlike Western feminists is true. They shied away from the very term "feminist" and from discussion of sexual issues. Indian men were not to blame, they reiterated; "custom" was the enemy and customs were the result of wars and imperialism. During the "Golden Age" Indian women had been accorded equality; the aim was to recreate the past rather than develop a totally new relationship between the sexes. The Indian social system was based on sex segregation but this did not have to result in inequality. Men and women, they believed, had different natures and different talents. This did not justify excluding women from certain professions or occupations, instead society should appreciate the special talents women had because they were nurturers and housekeepers. To play out a womanly role in the "world," not simply the "home," women needed education, physical freedom, and political-legal equality. For Western feminists, like the American journalist Grace Seton who visited India in 1925, it seemed that Indian women were working towards two contradictory goals. Their defense of the traditional "woman in the home" model seemed inconsistent with their desire to have women active in decision-making. Observing this specifically Indian brand of feminist, she wrote: "They may need to develop considerable skill as chariot drivers to make a successful race on those two mismatched horses."[36] But Indian women did not share all the assumptions of Western feminists. Hindu women looked back toward a "Golden Age," and lived in a world permeated with the concept of *shakti*, the "female generative force ... fundamental to all action, to all being in the Hindu universe."[37] Moreover, the joint family system provided many examples of the powerful matriarch. Indian women had images of female power and, in their struggle for women's rights, were reluctant to abandon these images for the Western feminist image of woman as powerless. They developed an ideology which emphasized women's strengths, and demanded for women a place in those arenas from which they had been excluded. Thus they did not denounce sex segregation as anathema to women's development.

Did these women succeed in improving conditions for Indian women generally? This question must be answered in the negative. Laws were made but they were rarely enforced; rights were granted but women had neither the education nor the necessary access to the legal system to take advantage of them. That child marriage still exists, only a few women fight legal battles to secure their inheritance, dowry prevails, and widows are stigmatized is not the fault of these early feminists who worked to change the system. It simply indicates that legal changes do not result in a changed social system. Sarojini Naidu, Kamaladevi Chattopadhyay, and many other women knew this when they pressed for legislation.

Looking back at the times in which they worked for social change, I think we should marvel that they dared and accomplished so much. Most of these women had grown up in purdah or at least in very sheltered environments. They temporarily left the protection of homes and families to work in the public arena—a behavior that was still suspect. They were dependent women—they lived with their families—and often had to tread very carefully to avoid alienating their relatives. These were not women with private incomes and independent identities; they were wives, mothers, daughters-in-law, and daughters with very few legal rights. In the end, their demands were accepted and formulated as law, giving the next generation the potential for greater independence and autonomy.

When I interviewed these women I found that many continued their work to improve women's position. Renuka Ray, a political activist, an advocate of divorce, and a tireless worker with the AIWC, in her 70s and 80s turned her attention to dowry issues and consumer rights. Romola Sinha worked throughout her life with the All Bengal Women's Union. The first home was designed to provide shelter for girls and women rescued by the police from brothels; later it housed refugees, runaways and battered wives as well as "rescued" women. These examples could be multiplied many times over. Many of the women who were activists in the 1930s remained active throughout their lives. Schneir and other Western writers should have looked more closely. If they had, they would have seen that behind the curtain there were "caged tigers," not slaves, and they became feminists.

The Politics of Respectability
Indian Women and the Indian National Congress

The early Indian National Congress decided to avoid topics associated with women's status and delegated education, child marriage, polygamy, purdah, and widowhood to the National Social Conference.[1] Nevertheless, women attended and took part in its earliest meetings. After Gandhi's rise to power in the Congress, social issues became an integral part of the party's platform and women were encouraged to join. Although their numbers were small and not representative of Indian women as a whole, they took a keen interest in political and social change. Unfortunately, many of those who have written on this period have opted for one of two simplistic views of the relationship between Congress and women. Either they are laudatory, claiming that Congress, particularly Gandhi, transformed Indian women;[2] or, they condemn Congress and Gandhi for manipulating women for political ends.[3] Neither captures women's experiences. The most active women combined an interest in politics and women's rights, often with the support of their husbands and families. To see them as puppets (led out of purdah into political agitation) or dupes (tricked or coerced into abandoning feminism for nationalism) denies the legacy of the nineteenth century, the intelligence of these women, and the complexity of their relationships with Congress. It also overlooks the way in which consciousness and ideology developed. For many women, political involvement spurred their feminism, while commitment to improving the status of women encouraged their involvement in the freedom struggle.

In this paper, I examine the interaction between the women who participated in the independence struggle and the Indian National Congress. Specifically, I consider the participation of women in the early Congress, Gandhi's program and his role in mobilizing women, and the institutions developed to bring women of the cities of Calcutta and Bombay into agitational politics from 1920 to 1922, and 1930 to 1932. My purpose is to establish a clearer understanding of the complex interrelationship that developed between the Indian National Congress, Gandhi, and women. My central argument is that the structures developed to mobilize women for the protest movement proved inadequate to the tasks of politicizing women, ensuring continued participation, or acting as channels for the expression of their interests. That these institutions developed as they did, with all their limitations, can best be understood as a function of the limited autonomy allowed women in a society which valued modesty and practiced sex segregation.

WOMEN AND THE EARLY CONGRESS

When Congress met in Bombay in 1889, there were ten women in attendance. These included Swarnakumari Devi, a well-known Bengali writer and editor of *Bharati;* Kadambini Ganguli, Bengal's first woman doctor; Pandita Ramabai, a social reformer, educationalist and noted Sanskrit scholar; and a number of Bombay women who were educated but less well known than these three. The following year, when Congress met in Calcutta, both Swarnakumari Devi and Kadambini Ganguli attended as delegates.[4] In 1901 a chorus of fifty-six girls representing all regions of India performed the song "Hindustan," written by Swarnakumari's younger daughter Saraladevi. The following year the Congress anthem was sung in Gujarati by Lady Vidyagauri Nilkanth and her sister Sharda Mehta.[5] This remained the Congress anthem until 1905 when Saraladevi sang Bankim Chandra Chatterjee's "Bande Mataram" [Hail to the Motherland] at the Benares session.

In addition to providing Congress with a few observers and delegates and the spirit of song, a number of Bengali women organized meetings and social events to further encourage women's interest in political and social issues. Saraladevi introduced festivals and rituals to celebrate Bengali heroes and arranged a *swadeshi* [things made in one's own country, in this case Indian-made items] exhibition for the Bombay Congress in 1904. In 1906, Kadambini Ganguli coordinated a Mahila Sammelan [Women's Conference] for the wives of Congress members gathered at the annual session held in Calcutta. Two years later, she organized a women's committee to support Gandhi's efforts in the Transvaal.[6]

Apart from attending Congress sessions and arranging women's meetings, women demonstrated their interest in political issues in other forums. In June 1899, *The Indian Social Reformer* reported that government representatives received a telegram from B. Rama Bai and a memorial signed by B. Amma Bai and other ladies, protesting the proposed abolition of the hospital in Manjeshwar. The article reported that the "ladies got their own way," the government vetoed the proposal to close the hospital, and approved its budget.[7]

A much larger group of women entered protest politics when Lord Curzon decided to partition Bengal. The boycott agitation received Congress approval at the Benares session of 1905. In addition to meetings, speeches, and petitions, the press and platform were used "to preach the new creed of radical nationalism," and reach an audience previously untouched by politics.[8] This new audience included Bengali housewives who were neither formally educated nor had the autonomy or leisure to regularly attend political gatherings. By linking *swadeshi* activities to popular religious observances, organizers persuaded large numbers of women to participate. For example, when Lilavati Devi, Hemangini Das, and Nirmala Sarkar introduced spinning wheels and looms into the homes of their neighbors, they urged women to spin enough every day to make their Durga Puja saris. Other women were encouraged to take the vow of *Meyer Kanta* [woman's chest] to daily set aside a handful of rice for the motherland. Thus women would be reminded of their duty to the nation, children would learn patriotism first-hand, and a storehouse of rice would be created.[9]

In another effort to modify traditional institutions to serve political ends, Ramendra Sundar Trivedi composed the Banga Lakshmi Bratakatha [the tale of the vow to Bengal's Goddess Lakshmi]. Meant to be read to women gathered to hear the story of Lakshmi and renew their vow to the goddess of fortune, this version explained the boycott and *swadeshi* in religious terms. On October 16, 1903 Trivedi's daughter read the *bratakatha* to an audience of 1000 women at the Vishnu temple in Trivedi's mother's village, Jemokandir, in Murshidabad district.[10] This *bratakatha* related how the goddess of fortune came to reside in Bengal and her threats to leave when the people neglected their duty. Her threats always recalled the people to their senses and reminded them of their duty to religion and society. The British made fools of the Bengalis by giving them cheap and shoddy products in exchange for items of value. The goddess was furious and decided to abandon Bengal forever. Upon hearing her decision, Bengalis wept and begged her to stay. This commotion annoyed the governor (a puffed-up fellow) who decided to separate brother from brother and Hindu from Muslim. Hoping to convince Lakshmi to stay, Bengalis took the vow of *swadeshi,* promising to no longer lust after foreign products and instead learn to live comfortably with the things they could make themselves. Hearing their vow Lakshmi agreed to stay in Bengal.[11]

On the day declared "Partition Day," October 16, 1905, the women of Bengal were asked to observe *arandhan* rites, that is, to observe a day without lighting the hearth and cooking food. That it was widely observed is borne out in women's accounts. Shudha Mazumdar recalled,

My first introduction to politics was in 1905 when I was seven years old and Mother served us with *phalahar* [fruit meal] when it was neither a fast-day nor a *puja* day. It was not a holy day nor did I hear of any holy purpose, so I was somewhat puzzled to notice the unusual silence in the kitchen and find that no fires were burning at all. On inquiry I learnt it was associated with the Swadeshi movement.[12]

Generally women were neither accustomed nor encouraged to attend public meetings. Not only were women of the respectable classes required to spend most of their time in the vicinity of their homes, the demands of food preparation meant they had little time to do other things. A non-cooking day made it possible for women to.be part of the political movement without overtly neglecting or leaving the household. However, on a few occasions women demonstrated publicly and when they did so, they made a great impression. The newspaper *Jugantar* reported that following the August 1907 sentencing of Bhupendranath Dutta to one year's rigorous imprisonment for preaching revolution, 200 women gathered at the home of Dr. Nilratan Sarkar to congratulate Bhupendranath's mother. Equally impressive was the appearance of Hemangini Das and a few other women at Nimtala *ghat* to witness the cremation of the patriot Brahmobandhab Upadhyay. Before the pyre was lit, Hemangini made a short speech about Brahmobandhab Upadhyay's ability to evoke the patriotism of women.[13]

These activities occurred in Bengal because it was the center of the *swadeshi* protest. However, there were a few sympathy protests by women in other areas, particularly the United Provinces and Punjab. Education, journalism, women's organizations, and a new spirit all contributed to the notion that women had a role to play in politics. Before World War I, their role was a supportive one. There were no women leaders, no women's political organizations, and no formalized integration of women into political institutions.

Our information about how many women were involved in ceremonies and demonstrations at this time is highly subjective. We read that 200 women were at the meeting to congratulate Bhupendranath Dutta's mother, that 1000 ladies gathered to hear the *bratakatha* at a temple in Trivedi's mother's village, that two women were delegates to the Indian National Congress in 1890, and that 56 girls sang at the Congress session in 1901, but beyond this there is very little data. Some authors have looked to British accounts for verification of women's participation in the *swadeshi* movement. J.C. Bagal cites an article by the wife of the British Prime Minister, which claimed women had been meeting in each other's homes and collectively vowing to buy only *swadeshi* products. Even though zenana [secluded] women do not always know how to read and write, she asserted, the *swadeshi* movement speaks to them and has an impact on their lives.[14] The journalist Valentine Chirol supported this view. He wrote in *Indian Unrest:* "the revolt seems to have obtained a firm hold in the zenana."[15] While it is possible to take these as indicators the movement among women was widespread, English people were terribly suspicious of the zenana simply because they did not control it. Just as conspiracies were thought to be hatched in dark narrow lanes, so the inhabitants of the impenetrable zenanas were suspected of nurturing dangerous political notions.[16]

Women's involvement in politics signaled the depth of patriotic feeling to both Indians and the British. For the British it was a danger signal; for Indians it added a new and poignant dimension to their cause. Children would be nurtured on patriotism, meals spiced with patriotism, and gods and goddesses worshipped with patriotic fervor. The emotional impact was great even if the numbers were small. In *Ghare Baire* [Home and the World], Rabindranath Tagore emphasized the danger associated with women's involvement in politics and ascribed that danger to women's lack of experience and knowledge of the larger world. This story underlined women's derivative status and limited impact. While women were powerful inspirational figures, they did not have the political power necessary to influence Congress policy or tactics.

WOMEN ENTER THE POLITICAL ARENA

Women entered agitational politics only after the First World War. This was made possible by a new infrastructure of women's organizations and the recruitment of women to existing political organizations. In the early years of the twentieth century, three women emerged as national leaders and provided inspiration for future generations. Two of these women were Indian: Madame Bhikaji Rustom K.R. Cama and Sarojini Naidu; and the third, Annie Besant, was British.

Madame Cama, born in 1875, was educated at Alexandra Native Girls' English Institution in Bombay, married a Parsi reformer, and moved to Europe in 1907. She was soon making the rounds of radical congresses accompanied by a well-known seditionist and in August unveiled an Indian national flag of green, yellow, and red bearing the words *Bande Mataram*. In her speeches, Madame Cama urged the "dumb millions of Hindus who are undergoing tyranny under the English capitalists and the British government" to imitate the Russians and overthrow their foreign rulers. She regarded the treatment of Indian women as an additional reason to overthrow the British tyrants. It is not clear how many in India were aware of her speeches and activities, but she made an impression on Indians studying and living in Europe. Perin Naoroji, one of Dadabhai Naoroji's[17] granddaughters studying in England, traveled to Paris to meet Madame Cama and became her traveling companion in 1910. Later, in the 1930s, Perin Naoroji Captain became a stalwart member of the Bombay Congress. By this time Indian women had elevated Madame Cama to the level of heroine and invoked her name, along with that of the Rani of Jhansi, in the their recitation of brave and politically active Indian women.[18]

Annie Besant was born in London in 1847 and had an extensive career behind her when she arrived in India to attend the 1893 annual conference of the Theosophical Society. Connected with a number of radical causes in England, Besant had written in 1874 that because women were expected to adhere to the law, they should be represented in the law-making process.[19] In India, she was overcome, for a time, by what *The Indian Social Reformer* called "a fit of spirituality," but then rallied and returned to issues that had interested her in England.[20] When Hindu College opened in Benares in 1901, Besant wrote about her plans to open a college for girls as one of the first steps in the process of regenerating Indian women. A few months later, she advocated sex segregation in modern institutions as a way of preserving India's ancient heritage. Do not follow the West, Besant cautioned her readers, rather look to your own past for models. "The ancient and wise way was training, educating and raising the women, putting her more and more on a high level, and then giving her a reasonable and dignified liberty."[21] *The Indian Social Reformer* chided her for her romantic view of ancient India. Hinduism, one journalist reminded its readers, did not look to the lives of gods and goddesses for models but rather took its rules of social behavior from the law codes. The practical question, this journalist concluded, was how to get women educated.[22]

By 1914, Besant had broken her 1894 vow to not enter politics and in the next few years became heavily involved in Indian politics. In 1915, Besant unveiled her plan to establish a Home Rule League and by September 1, 1916 the League was a fact. Speaking publicly and writing for her paper *New India*, she was seen as a threat to the government and asked to leave the country. When she refused, she was interned. Widespread protests gained her release and by August 1917 Besant had been elected President of the Indian National Congress. When the 1917 session of Congress met in Calcutta there were 400 women present. Unfortunately, Besant was exhausted by her recent experiences and spoke with less fire than had marked her earlier appearances.[23] In the same year she was named president of the Women's Indian Association and this newly formed organization dedicated itself to female franchise and social reform.

The youngest of these three women leaders was Sarojini Naidu, born Sarojini Chattopadhyay in Hyderabad in 1879. She traveled to England in 1895 to study first at King's College in London, and then at Girton College, Cambridge. In England she attracted the attention of a few literary figures who were charmed by her English poems and delicate appearance. She returned to India in 1898, married Captain M. Govinderajalu Naidu, Principal Medical Officer of the Gokinka Brigade with His Highness the Nizam's forces, and bore him four children.[24]

Sarojini Naidu attended her first session of Congress in 1904 when it met in Bombay. Because her father had established a Congress branch in Hyderabad, Sarojini was nurtured on the writings of India's great patriots. At Bombay she was finally able to meet some of the well-known nationalist leaders and a veteran of women's educational work, Ramabai Ranade. And, she was invited to recite her poem "Ode to India" before Congress. When Congress met in Calcutta in 1906, Sarojini's fiery speech so impressed Gokhale[25] that he urged her to dedicate her life to the country.

The next year she again spoke at Congress, and at the twenty-second session of the Indian National Social Congress (1908) she moved a resolution for the amelioration of the condition of Hindu widows. She spoke in favor of Karve's home and school[26] as model institutions to transform widows into useful and respected members of society. How could there be political freedom, she asked, when the country continued to suffer from this degrading "cancer"?[27] By this time she was clearly established as a forceful public speaker who linked the cause of India's freedom with the need to improve women's status.

Sarojini first met Gandhi in London in 1914. She had heard much about his campaign in South Africa and sought a meeting with him. Returning to India in 1915, she attended the Congress session at Bombay where she recited "Awake," a poem dedicated to Muhammad Ali Jinnah, that concluded with voices from all India's religions pledging their loyalty to the motherland.[28] By 1917, her political activities paralleled those of Annie Besant. In that year she spoke to Congress, supported the formation of the Women's Indian Association, and led the women's franchise delegation that met Undersecretary of State for India Edwin Montagu. At the 1918 Congress in Bombay, Sarojini moved a resolution to use the same test for women and men to determine eligibility to vote.[29]

By the end of the First World War, Indian women had been introduced to politics. An ideology evoking the "golden age" legitimized their political roles, while political tacticians had devised activities for women that preserved the ideology and norms of sex segregation. Perhaps most important, a few women leaders had emerged as inspirational figures. Besant and Naidu, leaders in Congress who linked improvement in women's status with nationalist aspirations, inspired other women to consider political involvement. However, neither Besant nor Naidu developed a program for women nor carved a place for women in the Indian National Congress. At this point, Gandhi appeared on the scene and forged a lasting connection between Congress and women.

It is difficult to pinpoint the origins of Gandhi's views on women for he was a pragmatic man rather than a systematic ideologue.

A.L. Basham claims Gandhi learned morality from his parents, the habit of calling on Rama from his nurse, and a faith in the power of asceticism from Hinduism. But his view of women and his insistence on the dignity of labor, Basham insists, came from Western sources. Basham contends that Gandhi first wrote about women as "helpmates" in 1898 during the first phase of the struggle in South Africa.[30] It was in South Africa, in 1906, that Gandhi decided to take the vow of *brahmacharya* [celibacy]. He argued this vow was an essential step in his effort to understand and respect, first, his wife, and second, all women. When he came to England to petition for the rights of Transvaal Indians (1906), he learned about the Suffragettes. The arrest and imprisonment of the eleven women who demonstrated in front of the House of Commons and refused to pay the fines, moved him to write "Deeds Better than Words" for *Indian Opinion*. He was impressed with these women who came from respectable families, he wrote, because they were willing to brave the insults of the streets and brutality of the police. During the next year, he followed and wrote about the Suffragette struggle. On one occasion, he discussed the propriety of men adopting "women's tactics." Gandhi believed the Suffragettes were demonstrating "manliness" and suggested that Indian men, if they imitated them, would not appear "effeminate," but strong for their refusal to accept oppression. It was only when the Suffragettes turned to violence that he lost sympathy with the movement.[31]

Gandhi's first long and well-developed speech on women in India was made in 1918 to the Bhagini Samaj.[32] Founded in 1916 in memory of G.K. Gokhale, this organization drew its membership from the Gujarati community. In his speech, Gandhi reminded the middle-class audience that 85 percent of Indian women lived in poverty and ignorance. The goal of the Bhagini Samaj should be to produce leaders who could work for social reform, female education, and new laws to give women their natural rights. These women leaders needed to be "pure, firm and self-controlled," he said, like the ancient heroines Sita, Damayanti, and Draupadi. They would be able to awaken women to understand that they were essentially equal to men, and had a right to freedom, liberty, and a supreme place in their own sphere of activity.[33] Equality did not mean that women would perform the same tasks as men, in Gandhi's ideal world men and women would "follow different vocations suitable to their different physical and emotional temperaments."[34]

NON-COOPERATION, 1920–1922

The Rowlatt Acts and the Amritsar massacre set the stage for the Non-Cooperation movement of 1920–1922. Gandhi first called for a *hartal* on March 30, 1919 and then changed the date to April 6. That day he addressed a meeting of "ladies of all classes and communities" and asked them to join the Satyagraha movement to facilitate the participation of their fathers, husbands, and sons in political activities.[35] In subsequent speeches he suggested specific activities for women. Gandhi urged women to take the *swadeshi* vow, that is, to promise to relinquish foreign goods and spend a certain amount of time each day spinning thread. He explained the need for this work in terms that women would understand but which also revealed his perception of women's proper role in society and the struggle for freedom. India's poverty, according to Gandhi, was a direct result of abandoning indigenous crafts and becoming dependent on foreign-made items. And women, key figures in India's regeneration, were ignorant of the causes of this poverty. To be able to save India, women must understand and be integrated into the world to play an equal role with men. In answer to the question of how this could be accomplished quickly, Gandhi urged rich and cultured women to take the vow to spin and thereby become models for the masses. In Bombay, a number of prominent women, including Lady Dorab Tata, Lady Petit, Ramabai Ranade, Lilavati Banker, and Mrs. Jerbanu Merwanji Kothawala, acted upon his suggestion and agreed to learn spinning.[36]

In urging women to become involved in political activities, Gandhi reminded them of Sita's sacrifice for the state. In a series of articles and speeches on the atrocities in Punjab, and particularly Amritsar, Gandhi explained to women that the British rulers were like the demon Ravana. It was in Punjab, the land of the *rishis* [saints], that Indians had been humiliated, in fact, made to crawl on their stomachs "like serpents." Living under Ravana Raj, the people were enslaved and slowly losing all sense of dharma [morality]. In these circumstances, women had both a religious and a civic duty to become like Sita. Just as Sita refused to forsake her husband and adorn herself for Ravana despite her great suffering, Indian women would have to make sacrifices. Only when women had joined men in the fight against this immoral government, could Rama Raj be re-established.[37]

This was a powerful message and different in content, although not in texture, from the earlier Bengali attempt to combine the *swadeshi* vow with the story of Lakshmi leaving Bengal. The trouble with the Rama-Sita analogy was the implications of Ravana's abduction and attempted rape of Sita. Fathers and husbands who accepted this identification of the British with Ravana, might become more protective of their womenfolk. Gandhi understood he was wielding a two-edged sword. He told his male audience to remember Sita's bravery when she was abducted and her ability to remain chaste even while a prisoner of Ravana. God, he reminded them, protects the honor of chaste women just as he protected Draupadi in the epic Mahabharata.[38]

Because Gandhi and other leaders sought to unite Hindus and Muslims in this movement, references to Hindu legends were not always appropriate. Appearing with Maulana Shaukat Ali[39] at a meeting in Patna, Gandhi significantly modified his message to women. Gone were references to Rama, Sita, Ravana, and Draupadi; women were urged to work harmoniously with one another, support the movement by spinning, and urge their husbands to join.[40] But on other occasions, when he denounced British rule as the rule of Satan and asked women to give up foreign cloth and learn to spin to save Islam, his speeches to Muslim women paralleled those to Hindu women. Spinning, he told an audience of women in Bombay, was the duty of every religious woman, whether Hindu or Muslim.[41] Smt. Ambujammal said Gandhi "touched the hearts of women." Gandhi, she said, told them their involvement in the movement was essential. Like goddesses and ancient heroines, they had an important role to play in saving society and would find the courage to do it. It was not necessary to abandon home and family to work in the movement, in fact, Gandhi urged women to "do what you can" even from the home.[42] He made women believe that they counted.

If Gandhi had not been sensitive to the attitudes of their guardians, it is unlikely he would have been successful in bringing women into the movement. Sucheta Kripalani believed he was able to mobilize women because he paid special attention to male attitudes: "Gandhi's personality was such that it inspired confidence not only in women but in the guardians of women, their husbands, fathers and brothers." Since his moral stature was high, "when women came out and worked in the political field, their family members knew that they were quite secure, they were protected."[43]

As the Non-Cooperation movement inaugurated at the special session of Congress in 1920 moved forward, it became clear that a number of women wanted to be more active in the protest movement than Gandhi had suggested in his speeches about the *swadeshi* vow. Congress declared April 6th to 13th, 1921 Satyagraha Week. Sarojini Naidu addressed a number of meetings in Bombay during that time, the last one attended by over 500 women. Those present decided to form the Rashtriya Stree Sangha, a women's political organization that would work closely with Congress but remain independent. Members of the Rashtriya Stree Sangha would join the District Congress Committee, collect money for the Tilak Swaraj Fund, and introduce women to the spinning wheel. Later in the year, the group was addressed by Urmila Devi, the widowed sister of the Bengali leader C.R. Das, who urged them to leave their homes and serve the country. In November, 1000 Bombay women demonstrated against the visit of the Prince of Wales.[44]

In Bengal, C.R. Das decided Congress volunteers would sell khaddar [handspun, handwoven cotton] on the streets of Calcutta to test the government's ban on Congress volunteers. Das' son was among the first batch of volunteers to be arrested; his wife, Basanti Devi, his sister, Urmila Devi, and his niece, Suniti Devi, were among the second. Subhas Bose, one of Das' greatest admirers, was shocked by his mentor's plan. With other young men, he protested that "no lady should be permitted to go out as long as there was a single man left."[45] But he soon became a convert. When word of this arrest spread, a huge crowd formed, composed of "Marwaris, Muslims, Bhattias, Sikhs, coolies, mill-hands and school boys," milled around until these women were released. One observer explained it was as if all womenfolk had been arrested. The next day, December 8, 1921, the whole city was in commotion. As for the women from the Das family,

they resumed picketing cloth shops and selling khaddar joined by numerous other lady volunteers, especially Sikh ladies; Calcutta students came out in hundreds, joined the prohibited volunteers corps, and marched out with khaddar on, seeking imprisonment. On that day, 170 were arrested.[46]

When he heard about events in Calcutta, Gandhi understood the potential of women's involvement in picketing. Writing in *Young India*, he suggested that women in other parts of the country follow the Bengal model.[47] It was clear that the arrest of a few prominent and well-respected women was sufficient to shame large numbers of men into joining the struggle. But it was not only men who were affected. There were 6000 ladies at the All-Indian Ladies Conference in Ahmedabad where Bi Amma ['The Mother'], the mother of Mohammad Ali and Shaukat Ali, spoke from the Congress *pandal*. She told those gathered that they must enlist as Congress volunteers and when their men had been sent to jail for protesting, fearlessly begin picketing to keep "the flag flying."[48] By January, women in Lahore, led by the principal of the Kanya Mahavidyalaya [Girls' School] of Jullundar, had begun picketing.[49] Sporadic demonstrations by women occurred in other cities, but Bombay and Calcutta were the main arenas for women's activism. Yet even in these cities, the women who protested and took part in political activities did so to inspire men or "to keep the flag flying." It was only in Bombay that a fledgling women's political organization existed.

Gandhi's message—be like Sita and spin, resonated with a handful of dedicated women who acted with the support of their male guardians. But these women, and their guardians, worried they might be confused with "women of the streets." Elite women appearing in public for the first time were terribly afraid of being confused with prostitutes. And, with good reason. C.S. Lakshmi noted that "in the 1921 movement in the Tamil region, the women who stood in the forefront in meetings were prostitutes who could face the public boldly,"[50] and this was true in other regions as well. In Barisal, East Bengal, 350 "fallen sisters" decided to join Congress, contribute from their earnings to the Tilak fund, and engage in Congress work. Gandhi wanted them to find another occupation and although most expressed their willingness to do so, neither Gandhi nor any other Congress leader could suggest an alternative. When Gandhi suggested they earn their living by spinning, they replied they could not earn enough money this way. Only eleven volunteered to try the experiment. Actually, Gandhi had no answer. Unable to present a viable alternative, he reiterated platitudes about the spinning wheel: "The wheel is a kind of wall for the protection of women. I cannot think of any other thing which may serve as a support for such sisters in India."[51] But this was no solution for either the women engaged in prostitution or for activists who wanted the freedom to move without opprobrium. For reasons closely related to his personal belief in the necessity of sexual restraint as a precondition to social and political reform, Gandhi wanted the "right kind" of women to lead the movement. As he had said in his earliest speeches, he wanted women from the higher classes to take the *swadeshi* vow because they could be models for other women. And, the participation of women from "respectable families" was possible only if they could engage in protests without creating scandal.

Following the suspension of Non-cooperation Movement in 1922, Gandhi turned to reconstruction. During the following years, he traveled extensively, spoke to numerous groups, and refined his position on women's role in public life. Speaking frequently to women's groups he repeated two messages: the best role model was Sita and spinning was an essential aspect of women's work.

Sita was a strong woman, Gandhi told his audiences. To call such a woman weak was to "murder language and violate dharma" for she had demonstrated her ability to withstand all assaults on her chastity.[52] As a young bride she had followed her husband into the forest, donned clothing made of tree bark, and given up all luxuries; later, as a prisoner of Ravana, she had resisted his attempts to seduce her. Sita had not recognized untouchability, he told women, nor had she been regional in her outlook. Gradually, mention of other heroines and goddesses receded from his speeches as he dwelt on Sita's virtues as appropriate for Indian women who would work to regenerate the nation.

Spinning could solve all India's problems. Unemployment would disappear when people spun and created demand for ancillary occupations such as carding and weaving. Spinning would bring discipline; discipline would make women pure in heart and soul and closer to the model woman Sita. Wearing homespun cloth, urban women would begin to identify with their poor village sisters. But the benefits envisioned by Gandhi went far beyond these changes associated with the physical acts of spinning and wearing homespun cloth. Somehow, spinning would break down regional prejudices and help eradicate a host of social customs which kept women backward—child marriage, enforced widowhood, and

Bharat Scouts. Students and teachers of Croswaithe Girls College Indianized the scouting movement. Allahabad, 1929 (Krishnabai Nimbkar Collection)

even prostitution. If this program was to be successful, women from the higher classes would have to devote their lives to this work and, in turn, influence other women.

Women's involvement would both uplift women and help solve India's problems. As women worked for *swaraj* [self-government], their problems would disappear. Even though Gandhi recognized that there were problems unique to women, he denied the possibility of conflict between the women's movement and the nationalist movement.

THE CIVIL DISOBEDIENCE MOVEMENT

When Gandhi returned to politics in 1928, he launched a movement that attracted large numbers of women. Women's participation in the Civil Disobedience movement of 1930–1932 differed quantitatively and qualitatively from their involvement in the early 1920s, and won them a place in history. It was the women's organizations and networks, developed between 1925 and 1930, that laid the groundwork for their positive reaction to Gandhi's call.

The activities of Bombay women received the most attention from the press, and rightly so since their demonstrations were the largest and their picketing the best organized. The explanation for this must be sought in a number of factors, including the cosmopolitan nature of the city, its transportation system, the presence of Parsis and Christians which accustomed people to the presence of respectable women in public places, and Gandhi's special appeal to Gujaratis with whom he shared language and culture.[53] The Rashtriya Stree Sangha, formed in response to Gandhi's appeal for a women's organization dedicated to *swaraj*, included Sarojini Naidu as president, Goshiben Naoroji Captain and Avantikabai Gokhale as vice-presidents, and Perin Naoroji Captain and Mrs. Ratten Behn Mehta as secretaries. The organization had two aims: *swaraj* and the emancipation of Indian women. These two goals were intertwined: *swaraj* would be achieved through peaceful means including spinning, and women's emancipation through political activities that included learning about the condition of the country, participating in "uplift" efforts, and acquiring organizational skills to run the Rashtriya Stree Sangha without male help. When the Tilak Swaraj Fund was set up, these women collected Rs. 44,519, which Gandhi then handed back to them for women's work. They used the money to set up the Khadi Vasthra Bhandar where 300 poor girls worked embroidering homespun cloth. They also planned khaddar exhibitions, created a school for the "depressed classes," and sold khaddar in the street.[54] While the reports comment on "hundreds of meetings for women" where lectures were given about the conditions of the country, no membership lists, exact dates of the meetings, or copies of the lectures have been preserved. Nevertheless, the leadership and structure of the Rashtriya Stree Sangha were sufficiently developed to spawn a new organization in 1930 and claim a membership of 700 women ready for action.

Following the Lahore Congress Conference of 1929, the Rashtriya Stree Sangha mobilized women for another assault on the British government. Its leaders, realizing that not all their members would be prepared to demonstrate, decided to form a separate volunteer corps for day-to-day work. This was the Desh Sevika Sangha and each member took an oath to spin and wear khaddar, in this case a saffron sari with a white blouse. Their saris were designed to evoke images of the brave Rajput women who sent their men to battle and then donned such saris before performing *jauhar* [suicide by fire] to avoid capture.[55]

Gandhi opened the Civil Disobedience campaign in March 1930 with his 240-mile march from Ahmedabad to Dandi to make salt in defiance of the British monopoly. Women asked to be included in this march[56] but Gandhi argued that if women joined, the British would call Indian men cowards who hid behind women.[57] Nevertheless, at every stop large numbers of women gathered to hear him speak. Police reports include accounts of meetings of 1000, 2000, and even 10,000. It is not clear that these audiences actually heard Gandhi's speeches for the reports indicate these were very noisy meetings. Gandhi spoke to the women about their duties: picketing liquor and toddy shops, boycotting taxed salt, and spinning and wearing khaddar.[58] Once the opening stage of Satyagraha, the march to Dandi, was over, women were fully incorporated into the movement. As Satyagraha spread to other parts of India, local Congress leaders placed no ban on women's participation.

Upon reaching Dandi, Gandhi convened a women's conference and unveiled his program for them.[59] They would concentrate on boycotting foreign cloth and liquor shops under their own leaders. Gandhi put women in charge of these two activities because he feared that if men picketed, there would be violence. On the basis of past experience, he concluded that only women had the patience necessary to perform these tasks. Women, according to Gandhi, could enter the hearts of men and transform them. As soon as he presented this program, members of the audience formed an organization for work in Gujarat with Ameena Tyabji as the president and Mithubehn Petit the secretary. This new organization would picket liquor and toddy shops and make personal appeals to shop owners to close their doors.[60]

Soon after this meeting, Gandhi published a pamphlet entitled "How to do the Picketing." Each picketing team was to be composed of nine women and a leader. Prior to picketing, the team would elect a delegation to meet the owner and request him to close his shop, if it sold liquor, or restrict sales, if he sold foreign cloth. Only when shopkeepers refused to comply, would the picketers appeal to potential customers. Gandhi required these women to always dress in a recognizable "uniform," carry banners, and whenever possible, sing *bhajans* [devotional songs]. In keeping with his concern that the picketers present themselves as "respectable" women, Gandhi prohibited obstructing customers and the use of abusive language. Men were to absent themselves, thereby reducing the potential for violence. Those women who were unable to picket could work from behind-the-scenes: encouraging their neighbors to spin and wear khaddar, and distributing propaganda. Finally, they should handle all accounts and receipts with care. Gandhi concluded this list with the statement: "The whole scheme presupposes on the part of men a genuine respect for women and sincere desire for their rise."[61]

Gandhi's speeches and publications gave women a clear and specific program of action, and they responded very quickly.

The Bombay Chronicle reported that "thousands of Gujarati women" demonstrated at the Chowpatty Sea Face and collected seawater in their brass and copper jugs.[62] Women volunteers picketed toddy shops, asking the owners to close and the patrons to leave,[63] while other women sold salt and carried on an intensive house-to-house campaign for *swadeshi*.[64]

Much of this activity had been organized by the Desh Sevika Sangha, which took over the task of designing and supervising the picketing campaign. At first, picketing seemed an exciting activity and Desh Sevika Sangha membership rose to 560. Before long, it became clear this number included many "ornamental *sevikas*" and membership dropped, remaining stable at about 300. These women were asked to place themselves in one of four categories: A—prepared to picket toddy shops, face public insult, and go to jail; B—prepared to picket cloth shops and be arrested, but unwilling to face assault or go to jail; C—prepared to go house-to-house to preach *swadeshi* (this was considered especially appropriate for women with young children); and D—willing to go house-to-house to teach spinning.[65]

While the Desh Sevika Sangha found "ornamental *sevikas*" something of a nuisance, the "wrong kind" of woman posed a more serious problem. After they were approached by "undesirable women," Desh Sevika leaders made it clear that they wanted to recruit only from the "good classes." According to Goshiben Captain this was essential if the picketers were to demand respect from the public. Women picketers must preserve their "dignity and innate modesty," she insisted, and this would be impossible if they were marching side-by-side with women of "undesirable" character or even "leftists" who suggested tactics such as lying in the doorways of foreign cloth shops. Theoretically, the Desh Sevika Sangha was open to all women willing to take the vow and follow orders, but in actual fact, membership was strictly controlled. Females over the age of eighteen were eligible to apply but the committee could "refuse to admit any person without disclosing the reason to the applicant."[66] Goshibehn, like so many other women leaders of the time, was more concerned with modesty than sisterhood. Sentenced to prison for three months in 1935, she was horrified to find her cellmate was a prostitute. Characterizing these women as "low-class" and diseased, she reported that she and her fellow *sevikas* judiciously avoided association with them.[67]

By May, the *sevikas* had begun picketing and Sarojini Naidu was to lead the raid on the Dharasana Salt Works. She led the protest on May 15, 1930, was arrested, and released. On the 21st of May, Sarojini led the second batch of raiders, was arrested, and this time jailed for almost a year. Sarojini's presence at the Dharasana Salt Works and the picketing carried on in the city, attracted considerable attention. Those who witnessed women's actions were inspired. Kamaladevi Chattopadhyay, who watched the 21st May scene, tried to capture the magic of that day:

But they (the *satyagrahis*) were brave. They watched their leader sitting with an unfailing smile on her lips, occasionally breaking into rippling humor, giving an encouraging glance here and a sweet look there. They watched her with amazement as she cheered and heartened them. . . . She was a delicate poetess who had spent her days rhyming tender verse. Yet here Sarojini Naidu sat, at perfect ease, as much a queen of this burning sandy world as she had been of her luxurious mansion.[68]

Equally impressive were the picketing and the processions organized by the Desh Sevikas. Many foreign-cloth merchants, faced with the threat of lady picketers, signed a pledge not to sell foreign cloth until an honorable peace had been arranged for the country.[69] People were astonished to read about processions that included 1000 to 2000 women. The demonstration arranged to celebrate Gandhi's birthday and ask for the release of Lilavati Munshi, Perin Captain, and Mrs. Lukanji, was a mile-long chain of women led by saffron-clad *sevikas* carrying placards. It was estimated the procession itself included more than 5000 women with a crowd of over 10,000 assembled at either end. The placards and the speeches emphasized themes that were associated with women's participation in the movement: communal harmony, Gandhi's undisputed leadership, loyalty to Congress, and the identification of *swaraj* with female emancipation.[70] Bombay made headlines all over the country and the Congress organizers in other areas were encouraged to emulate their model. The participation of women proved this was a successful movement with "firm public support," and gave a significant boost to morale in the days following Gandhi's arrest.

But Gandhi's view of women's participation and their right to make their own decisions was not shared by other Congress leaders. When he asked Sarojini to lead the raid at Dharasana, some of his colleagues argued the situation was too dangerous and that her presence was more urgently needed elsewhere. Gandhi was adamant and Sarojini declared "the time had come when women must share equally the sufferings and sacrifice of their men comrades in the struggle for the liberation of their country."[71] When he asked women to participate in public demonstrations, Gandhi told them to plan their own work and not let men tell them what to do.[72] But other Congress leaders thought otherwise and less than one year after Desh Sevika Sangha led spectacular processions in Bombay, they were told Congress planned to form a new organization to carry on women's work. At this time, the INC was revamping its constitution to increase control over volunteers. Nehru wanted the Desh Sevikas to seek formal recognition but he was also interested in the formation of a Women's Department within Congress. While this would have represented a significant step forward in terms of the integration of women and women's issues into the Congress structure, the Desh Sevika Sangha jealously guarded its independence.

Goshiben immediately wrote to Sardar Patel, Joint Honorary Secretary of the Bombay Provincial Congress Committee, arguing there was no need for a new organization since the Desh Sevika Sangha had been formed for this purpose and had always consulted with the BPCC about its work. She concluded by asking for a "clear mandate" regarding Desh Sevika work and Patel agreed to place her letter before the council. At this point K.F. Nariman, the Bombay Congress leader, stepped in as mediator and proposed the Desh Sevika Sangha be recognized as a Congress organization. Nehru replied this would be possible only if its organizational structure conformed to certain rules and the training of volunteers be taken more seriously. In the end, Nariman won and the Desh Sevika Sangha was recognized by the Working Committee as a

"Corps within the meaning of the Hindustan Seva Dal." However, it was decided that rule number 14, that picketers had to be given special training, did not apply.[73]

The reorganization scheme had been designed to curb unruly elements within Congress. Even though some leaders would have liked more control over the Desh Sevikas, women did not constitute a major threat to Congress rule. On another level, the goal of reorganization was to integrate Congress' various constituencies. The leaders of the Desh Sevika Sangha failed to see the advantages associated with closer involvement with Congress. They successfully blocked the formation of a viable women's department and retained control of their informal sex-segregated political organization.

After the Desh Sevika Sangha had been given its mandate, the issue of who made decisions continued to surface. Since it was impossible to affect only foreign-cloth shops when picketing and to picket all markets equally, their activities hurt innocent businesses in targeted markets while foreign-cloth shops flourished in other markets. By the summer of 1931, a number of "patriotic merchants" had complained to Congress. Sardar Patel spoke to Desh Sevika leaders about the problem and suggested they devote more attention to *swadeshi* activities and less to closing shops. They assured him they would do their best but when Patel spoke with a body of merchants he felt it necessary to ask the merchants to be patient.[74] Gandhi's plan of action for women, seen as uniquely suited to their temperament and talents, had been bold and exciting and women successfully carried it out. But instead of using their new power to demand representation at various levels in the Indian National Congress, they remained independent and continued to cooperate despite minor tensions.

The end of December 1931 saw Gandhi return from the Round Table Conference in London and his immediate arrest. The government declared Congress, the Rashtriya Stree Sangha, and the Desh Sevika Sangha illegal. The leaders of the Rashtriya Stree Sangha and Desh Sevika Sangha dissolved their organizations and gave their funds and records to the "First Sevika" who was to pass them to the next in line if she were arrested. Meanwhile, they resumed vigorous picketing of the market, called public meetings, and distributed a flood of pamphlets. As predicted, leaders were arrested and jailed, and leadership was passed to the next in line. Even with dwindling numbers and increasingly dangerous conditions, women continued to picket. The accounts of these days reveal that violence was just below the surface and communal tensions high. On some occasions, the crowd protected the women from the police, but on other occasions it was the police who protected the women from the crowd. The work of the Desh Sevika Sangha was suspended following the Hindu-Muslim riots of 1932. After Gandhi's fast against the untouchable award in 1932, members of the Rashtriya Stree Sangha and Desh Sevika Sangha formed yet another organization. With many of the old members present, the Gandhi Seva Sena emerged in 1932 to work for communal harmony and Harijan uplift.[75]

Bengal, like Bombay, was a province where women were active during the Civil Disobedience movement of 1930–1932. As was true in Bombay, the foundation of their participation in the 1930s had been laid in the 1920s. In Bengal, decision making was shared between women and Congress leaders, there were more "feeder organizations," and a thinner line between violence and non-violence. The difference between women's participation in the two cities can be explained in terms of the differences in leadership and politics, as well as the physical layout of the cities, and socio–economic and cultural factors. In both provinces women were touched by Gandhi's words and program, formed their own political groups, and were not included in Congress policies and institutions.

The Mahila Rashtriya Sangha, the first organization to mobilize women for political work, was begun in 1928. Subhas Chandra Bose approached Latika (nee Ghosh) Bose after she successfully organized a women's demonstration against the Simon Commission and asked her to form a new organization. At first she was reluctant to accept the offer. A graduate of Oxford University, she knew that joining Congress would destroy whatever chance she might have of securing a position in the Educational Service. In the end, Subhas prevailed and Latika agreed to join Congress and form the Mahila Rashtriya Sangha.[76]

Latika selected Subhas' mother, Prabhabati Bose, to be president and his sister-in-law, Bivabati, to be vice-president of the Mahila Rashtriya Sangha. Subhas wanted Basanti Devi, veteran of the Non-Cooperation movement, as president but Latika disagreed, arguing that Basanti Devi was considered too westernized by most Bengali women. Not only was Prabhabati orthodox, she could be introduced as "Ma," the mother of Bengal's most popular nationalist leader, Subhas Chandra Bose. With Prabhabati's consent, Latika used ten neighborhood educational groups to form the nucleus of the organization.[77]

The Mahila Rashtriya Sangha, much like the Rashtriya Stree Sangha in Bombay, wanted both *swaraj* and the improvement of women's status. These two goals were inseparable according to Mahila Rashtriya Sangha leaders who argued the nation could never be free unless women's lives improved and improving women's lives depended on freedom from foreign domination. The first step toward *swaraj* involved educating women about the realities of India's condition and their condition as women. In articles designed to mobilize women, Latika explained India's poverty and the appropriate remedies in terms that combined Gandhi's message with ideas in Trivedi's special *bratakatha*. She charged women to wake up and take a good look at their surroundings. They would see a poor country but it had not always been poor, she wrote. At one time, India was renowned for its arts and crafts, revered for the scholarship of its universities, and famous for its great leaders. Now, under foreign domination, people were poor, crafts had been replaced by foreign-made items, and leaders were weaklings. Meanwhile, women stayed indoors and closed their eyes to its poverty. What was to be done, she asked. Was there any power left in the people? Remember the tales our grandmothers told us, wrote Latika, the tales of the *devas* [lower-level deities] and the *asuras* [powerful beings opposed to the *devas*]. Just as the *devas* were losing, Durga appeared as Shakti. Women must remember they were the Shaktis of the nation. They needed to recall stories of brave Rajput queens who sent husbands and sons into battle and then prepared for their own death. Like the heroines of old, modern women had to realize the

Shakti within themselves and, like sparks, ignite the fires that would leave people purified and ready to serve the motherland.[78]

In recruiting for the Mahila Rashtriya Sangha, Latika first asked male Congress leaders for the names of likely recruits. Because family approval and support for women's activities was essential for the success of this venture, Latika approached women whose fathers, brothers, or husbands were involved with Congress or the revolutionary movement.[79] Teaching women about the need for independence was to be carried out in *shakti* mandirs that would also teach literacy, mothercraft, first-aid, and self-defense. Latika and others who wanted to build women's political organizations understood that women were totally isolated from the affairs of the country.[80] They knew that unless ordinary women began to see themselves as part of the nation, they would not be willing to make personal sacrifices.[81]

Latika's organizational skills and flare for the dramatic were evident when she organized women to march, alongside men, in the Congress parade of 1928. Subhas Bose wanted female volunteers to march, like men, in military uniforms at the opening of the Congress session in Calcutta. "Colonel" Latika was asked to recruit and lead the girls. She managed to assemble 300 young women from Bethune College and Victoria Institution, and from among the Calcutta Corporation teachers. There were many debates about their involvement. Different leaders took positions on whether or not the young women would wear trousers, stay in the camp at night, and march in the regular procession or simply serve at tea stalls and do other work to make the session run smoothly. Latika always argued for the trappings of modesty— "uniforms" of dark green saris with red borders worn over white blouses, the colors of the Congress flag, instead of trousers and no females in camp at night, but she stood her ground on the issue of women marching in the regular procession. Although she confessed she made a poor Colonel, failing to stay in step and salute correctly, she wanted female volunteers to appear as the equals of men in the struggle for freedom.[82] The marching girls had an electric effect. According to one press report:

It was itself a sufficient indication that henceforward whenever the clarion call for National Service would go forth—there would come as spontaneous and enthusiastic a response from the mothers and sisters as from the manhood of this country. The ladies of Bengal are no longer content with applauding their fighting brethren from afar but are determined to render what they can in the active service of the Motherland. They want to be in the thick of the fight. As the ladies clad in their saris marched past to the sound of the bugle and the beating of the drum, there could be traced not a touch of all the frailties that are so commonly attributed to them. No faltering, no hesitancy, no softness associated in popular minds with the womanhood of Bengal but chivalry written on every face and manifest in every movement.[83]

Women were visible through the entire Congress session. After the opening parade, they manned the tea-stalls, helped with local arrangements, and attended the All-India Women's Social Conference held in conjunction with Congress meetings. The conference was presided over by Her Highness the Maharani (Jr.) of Travancore and debated resolutions on dowry, female education, and divorce. Those present agreed that dowry, not a custom during India's "Golden Age," created humiliating conditions for girls. Discussing female education, they lamented that so little was being done and urged government to allocate more funds. Then came the most controversial topic—divorce. Although she had been asked not to mention this topic, Renuka Ray denounced the existing system and demanded equal rights for men and women in marital life. Her resolution, urging support for Sir Hari Singh Gour's divorce bill, was passed. In deference to the conservative members of the conference, most newspapers decided not to report this part of the meeting.[84]

Despite the discomfort of some Congress leaders, the 1928 session set a precedent for the involvement of Bengali women in political activities. Women marched side-by-side with men in demonstrations and spoke publicly about women's problems. Unfortunately the volatile political situation made it difficult to gain support for women's issues.[85]

In response to the Congress call in 1929 for groups of women to serve the cause, Calcutta women formed the Nari Satyagraha

Samiti. Urmila Devi became its president, Jyotirmoyee Ganguli vice-president, Santi Das secretary, and Bimal Protiba Devi joint-secretary. Urmila Devi had been named president because of her long association with Gandhi and her galvanizing arrest in 1921. However, she represented an earlier generation, and was not very active. The core group included fifteen to twenty women able to picket regularly and risk going to jail. They were all educated, from professional families and had, until this time, observed a form of modified purdah. In terms of marital status they were diverse, the group included single women, married women, and widows. The early Samiti was composed entirely of Bengali women from the Brahmin, Kayastha and Vaidya castes, but they were later joined by women from other communities. They chose white khaddar saris as their picketing uniform.[86]

Santi Das, the secretary of Nari Satyagraha Samiti, was one of its most important members. She had inherited her daring from her mother. Asokalata, the daughter of a Brahmo missionary, who was among the first women to pass the Bethune College entrance examination. Asokalata's advanced notions on female education were not shared by her husband. When he opposed sending their daughters to Calcutta University, Asokalata left him and educated her daughters herself. Santi took her MA at Calcutta University and then opened a school, Deepali Shiksha Mandir, in their home with the help of her mother and sister.[87]

Santi recruited her own students and Calcutta Corporation schoolteachers for the Nari Satyagraha Samiti. Women were willing to join, they told her, because they knew the movement needed them. They had witnessed the police beating male protesters, and thought that if they had intervened, this would not have happened.[88] Calcutta newspapers reported many incidents involving women in 1930 but the numbers involved were few in comparison with Bombay. Sometimes 200 to 300 women were mobilized but more frequently, demonstrations were held with 15 to 25 women present. But numbers are not always a good indicator of impact. In Bombay, Gandhi asked men to stay away from picketing women, but this was rarely the case in Calcutta. When twenty-two ladies from the Samiti were arrested in July of 1930, shopkeepers in Burrabazar immediately closed their shops fearing violence from the crowd.[89] A few days later, four ladies sitting on some bales of foreign cloth deterred coolies from moving the bales.[90] Those picketing were "respectable women," and the watching crowds would have exploded in violence had the police molested them. Sensing this, the police learned to treat the women with respect while they *lathi*-charged the crowd.

The threat of violence was never far from the surface in these demonstrations. By May and June, the Civil Disobedience campaign had unleashed some very un-Gandhian ways of fighting the British. By October, the British retaliated with special ordinances which made it possible for them to search and detain without reasonable suspicion. Magistrates now had special powers and it became more and more dangerous to be involved with any political movement. As the police ordinances were rigorously applied, fewer women demonstrated and more women became active revolutionaries. Bina Das and others have suggested there was a cause-effect relationship; they joined the revolutionaries because they wanted to advance the cause of independence and because other channels were closed to them. By 1931, Bengal was declining as a center for non-violent political activity, while women revolutionaries became famous for assassinations, daring raids, and political dacoity.[91]

The intensity of the times, the activities of women, and the difficulty of garnering any attention for women's issues gave rise to a demand for a separate women's Congress in Bengal. In the first week of May 1931, Santi Das, acting as convener for the planned Congress, requested women to send ten delegates from each district to the meeting. In preparation for the Calcutta gathering, Congress women held district meetings and discussed the need for social reform.[92] When they arrived in Calcutta, the delegates were met by young volunteers wearing crimson khaddar saris, ushered to their seats, and treated to a speech by the grand old lady of politics and feminism, Saraladevi Chaudhurani. While the district conferences voiced platitudes about Indian womanhood and their great awakening during the Civil Disobedience movement, Saraladevi's speech hit hard.

Saraladevi explained that a separate Congress for women was necessary because women, from their earliest childhood (when they were denied the sweets which were given to their brothers), had been treated as separate and inferior. The sexes were interdependent but,

men exploited women far more for their own purposes than helped them in realizing their needs. The woman's feeling has never been the man's, neither the woman's point of view his. In giving expression to this deep seated conviction at last and asserting themselves, the women of Bengal have come on a line with the women of other countries.[93]

Discussing the entry of women into political affairs, Saraladevi acknowledged that men had encouraged them to join. However, there were few among these men who cared about improving the lives of women. Women who had participated in the movement could expect flowery speeches but not appointment to subcommittees and councils. Summing up women's experience with politics she said that Congress had "assigned to women the position of law-breakers only and not law-makers."[94] To change the situation, women needed to demand equal treatment and equal status. They needed to join together so that leaders like Nehru, who concerned themselves with peasants and workers, would begin to focus on "teeming womenfolk." If women were to demand fair and equal treatment from Congress, then Congress might well have an anti-brothel campaign, she told her audience. Congress regarded drinking liquor harmful to men and asked that toddy shops be picketed and boycotted. Why wasn't the same done to brothels? Saraladevi asked. Weren't brothels as harmful and destructive to women?[95] Saraladevi concluded what was certainly the most forceful feminist speech of the 1930s with a list of women's demands. Women's ten "Fundamental Rights" included: equal inheritance, equal rights to guardianship, no sex discrimination, fair wages, punishment for sex-related crimes, closing brothels, compulsory primary education, adult education, female teachers in co-educational institutions, and adult franchise. At the end of the speech she urged women to also remember the message of the

Gita, and seek purification through political work. While engaged in political work and efforts to improve women's status, it was women's responsibility to conserve India's civilization.[96]

While only a few delegates supported Saraladevi's feminism and plan of action, they agreed with her views on the vote. Saraladevi wanted universal adult franchise without any special conditions, but there were other women who thought separate electorates would benefit them. Some wanted separate electorates to preserve their "special" sex-segregated status, while others, like Santi Das, believed separate electorates would give women a chance to express their needs. It had been her "bitter experience," she said, that when men and women worked together, "the former invariably dominated the show with the result that the latter could not get proper facilities to contribute their share." But support for separate electorates never gained sufficient backing and the delegates passed a resolution in favor of adult franchise. Other resolutions requested the release of détenus, commutation of death sentences given to Bengali and Punjabi revolutionaries, and the organization of Desh Sevikas to work in the mofussil. These final resolutions were neither exciting nor feminist. Resolutions in support of allowing inter-caste and inter-racial marriage, birth control, and equal treatment of women in insurance plans did not pass.[97] Nor did the plan to form a Women's Congress bear fruit. In Bengal's highly charged Political environment, women's issues were swept aside. Women remained outside the existing political institutions and without a political organization of their own.

CONCLUSIONS

The activities of women in Bombay and Calcutta tell only a partial story of women's participation in the struggle for independence. While the pattern was similar in other cities, this does not tell us anything about women's involvement in rural areas. What do we know about rural women?[98] We know how many Indian women were convicted (see Table 1), but these figures only confirm that their numbers were small. The volumes that list the freedom fighters in various provinces, for example those on the United

Province, refer to women as "Kamla Devi" or "Maya Devi," sometimes adding they were "the daughter of ... ," or "the wife of ... . " In those few cases where more information is available, one learns about the woman's village and membership in Congress. We are left with the impression that many joined the movement with their male guardians but without more information, we simply do not know. Their participation undoubtedly helped rally others to the cause, but they neither formed political organizations of their own nor gained positions of power in Congress.[99]

In an attempt to gain some understanding of the rank and file, I interviewed four women from Udipi, Karnataka, who were convicted and served prison sentences between 1931 and 1942. Their motivations for joining the movement were different and political considerations played only a small role in their decisions to take action. The two stories which follow illustrate this point.

Kamala Adhikari said that her husband had read about the Salt Satyagraha in high school but was not able to join Congress until 1936. In 1938, he became Chairman of the Taluk Congress and after hearing Gandhi say women would have to take part in the struggle, "told" her to join the movement. Kamala obeyed her husband and accepted freeing the country from slavery as a religious duty. When her husband went to prison in 1940, he took the *mangalsutra* [the necklace worn by married women] from her neck, symbolically releasing her to put her duty to the country first. Unused to leaving the house, she simply went and stood in front of the Jaina temple until arrested. She was sentenced to Cuddalore Central Gaol for six months. When she returned from prison, she resumed her household duties and neither went to meetings nor participated in constructive work. She reported that the experience of offering satyagraha and going to prison had not effected much change in her life.[100]

Ambabai had been married at age twelve and gone to live in Bombay in 1920. In Bombay a member of the Bhagini Samaj told her about Gandhi, Tilak, and *swaraj*, and taught her to spin. Widowed at sixteen, Ambabai returned to Udipi to live in her father's house and "sit in the God room." Bored with a life dedicated to prayer, her health suffered and she had irregular menses. Then she dreamed that Krishna came to her, ran his hands over her body, and said, "Do not be afraid, as long as I am here I will take care of you." Taking this as a sign, she joined those picketing foreign-cloth and toddy shops. With others, she made and sold salt. The first time she was arrested the magistrate released her, but when she was arrested the next day, she was sentenced to four months in prison. Instead of finding imprisonment a dreadful experience, Ambabai enjoyed it and gained weight. After her release, Congress leaders asked her to speak locally about the importance of spinning and wearing khaddar, and at the annual car festival, about the evils of alcohol. She happily carried out these activities and, for three months led *prabhat pheries* [morning singing processions]. Ambabai regarded these as the happiest days of her life.[101]

What do we learn from this evidence? First, that we know very little about women's participation in the nationalist movement once we move outside the major urban areas. We have records (scanty as they are) of the women's organizations of Bombay and Calcutta but few records of many of the women in towns and villages who were convicted and went to prison. In fact, we know very little about "women" and the Indian National Congress, and only something about those women who became leaders of associations and organizations during the nationalist period.

The tendency to focus on women as a collectivity rather than on specific groups of women is one of the legacies of the independence struggle. Gail Pearson has argued that nationalist leaders consciously manipulated the word "women" to suggest the "participation of a united social universe."[102] For contemporary historians, this generalized category operates against understanding the relationship of different groups of women with Congress.

There was a vast gap between well-educated women from families that began to experiment with women's modernization in the nineteenth century, and less-educated women who responded to their "dual duty"—to their beloved Gandhi and to their guardians who invited them (or ordered them) to join. It was only in urban areas that organizations were able to blend feminist and nationalism. Since the early years of the twentieth century, there were a few women who argued that associations dominated by men

overlooked women's concerns. To counter this situation they formed
their own women's organizations—led by women—to discuss
women's problems. Faced with the need for disciplined action
during the nationalist movement, they borrowed from this model
and formed women's political organizations. The organizations
were safe havens for women newly emerged from purdah because
they operated in harmony with society's conventions of female
modesty. The less-educated women generally followed men, and
the data suggests that if participation had a long-range impact on
their lives it was not in the realm of politics.

Even when women determined their own political agenda, they
did so with the permission of male guardians, clothed in symbolic
saris, and under the protection of a women's organization. It was
the leaders of these organizations who decided to restrict membership
to "respectable" women and insist their members conform to
standards of modest behavior. By doing so, they undermined their
claim to speak for all women and stalled the development of a
strong women's movement. But this was not a male or Congress
plot to "control" women, these leaders were concerned with their
image and rightly so, for they lived in a society unaccustomed to
seeing middle class women in the streets.

Unfortunately, a strong connection was never forged between
the women who joined the nationalist movements and the leaders,
other than Gandhi, of the Indian National Congress. Gandhi told
women "do what you can," and many believed that spinning at
home made them part of the nationalist movement. Gandhi also
told them they would be fully integrated into the country's political
bodies after independence, but he could not speak for other political
leaders. When the elections of 1937 were announced, activist
women expected Congress to support them in safe constituencies.
Congress bosses decided otherwise, and chose party men over
women without power and influence in the provincial Congress
Committees.

Finally, we have to ask whether or not the various ideologies
that motivated women's participation could have resulted in a
feminist women's department or women's platform acceptable to
Congress. Gandhi believed in women's strength and moral equality

with men, but urged them to participate in political movements by evoking goddesses, not by talking about basic rights. Urban women leaders were educated and influenced by an ideology of women's rights and even feminism, yet few of them dared to speak what they believed about sensitive issues such as divorce and birth control. Some, like Renuka Ray, supported Gandhi and, at the same time, wrote and argued for radical reform. Others, like Latika Ghosh, linked religion and politics when they spoke to women. The women's associations formed to mobilize women made their primary goal independence and postponed women's rights until later. At this time, many Congress leaders shared the view that women's proper place was in the family, under male protection. Under these circumstances, the only women's movement that could emerge was one sheltered by the umbrella of respectability.

Table 1: "Convictions for Civil Disobedience, 1932–1933"[103]

Province	Total convicted	Convicts as percentage of population	Women	Women as percent-age of total convicts
Madras	3,490	0.007	291	8.34
Bombay	14,101	0.064	939	6.66
Bengal	12,791	0.026	776	6.07
UP	14,659	0.030	656	4.48
Punjab	1,774	0.008	121	6.82
B & O	14,903	0.040	370	2.48
CP	4,014	0.026	299	7.45
Assam	1,271	0.015	93	7.32
NWFP	6,053	0.250	0	0
Delhi	1,048	0.165	66	6.29
Coorg	269	0.165	9	3.35
Ajmer-Merwara	298	0.053	9	3.02
Totals	74,671		4859	4.86

"Women of Character, Grit, and Courage"
The Reservation Debate in Historical Perspective[1]

The 81st Constitutional Amendment to the Indian Constitution, a proposal to reserve one-third of the seats in the Lok Sabha and state legislatures for women, is usually discussed without reference to colonial debates about reservations. When women first asked for the vote, they were not concerned with universal franchise, rather their aim was to secure the vote for at least some women. Limited numbers gained the right to vote between 1921 and 1930 when provincial legislative councils voted to add women to the list of voters enfranchised by the India Act of 1919. In 1927, the British began to gather evidence for a new India Act. This initiated the second round in the fight for the vote, a struggle that witnessed a demand for reserved seats. Some women, dissatisfied with their meager representation, saw reservations as a solution to the problem, while others stood firm with the Indian National Congress, demanding universal franchise. The arguments of this period are especially relevant today because they played a role in women's disavowal of reservations during the Constituent Assembly and, in fact, until the 1970s. As Mary John has pointed out in her insightful article on the reservation debate and the women's movement, Indian feminists have only recently begun to look favorably at the possibility of reservations.[2]

EARLY WOMEN'S ORGANIZATIONS

Indian women's interest in the vote came much later than their efforts to promote education, the end of harmful social customs, and participation in public life. The earliest women's organizations, either begun by men or set up as ladies' branches of men's organizations, expressed no interest in representation on the councils and boards that first gave Indian men a say in how they were governed. These women's organizations and those begun in the early twentieth century were dominated by "new women," the recipients of reformist male attention in the late nineteenth century. While these organizations brought women together to formulate their demands and initiate projects to help unfortunate women, the desire to form women-only organizations did not lead to an interest in political representation. The women who belonged to these organizations were elitist, rarely challenged patriarchy, and accepted the political stance, whether pro-British or nationalist, of their menfolk.[3]

They were members of the elite by dint of their fathers' and/ or husbands' educational and professional attainments, not their own, and while they belonged to the higher castes, they did not all have wealth or property. To understand their complicity, it is helpful to refer to Judith Walsh's distinction between "new patriarchy" and "old patriarchy." Whereas the old joint family defined women's roles in terms of child-bearing and family duties, new patriarchy wanted educated women, capable of making decisions, to regard their husbands (not the head of the joint family) as supreme.[4] These women followed and assisted their husbands; the wives of civil servants appeared at bridge parties and prize-giving ceremonies underscoring the benevolence of British rule, while the wives and daughters of nationalists attended the annual meetings of the Indian National Congress as delegates or to sing patriotic songs. Although many of them expressed an interest in politics and wanted women-only organizations, they did not ask for political representation.

THE FIRST DEMAND FOR FRANCHISE

The first step towards politics came in 1917 when a delegation of Indian and British women applied for an audience with Secretary of State Edwin Montagu. These women had wanted to discuss education and social reform but because Montagu met only with political delegations, they asked for an audience to present their political demands. In this meeting, they asked that women be accorded the status of "people" in a self-governing nation within the Empire.[5]

The Indian National Congress immediately endorsed women's request for the franchise on the same terms as men, the property qualification. At a special session of Congress (1918), Sarojini Naidu told her colleagues that extending the vote to women was rational, scientifically and politically sound, compatible with tradition, and consistent with human rights. Referring to the objection that politics would make women less feminine, she explained,

We ask for the vote, not that we might interfere with you in your official functions, your civic duties, your public place and power, but rather that we might lay the foundation of national character in the souls of the children that we hold upon our laps, and instill into them the ideals of national life.[6]

Naidu's belief, that women were fundamentally different from men and should be heard because of their special knowledge, fit neatly with the reformist platform that envisioned women as men's helpmates.

Following Congress endorsement of female franchise, women's organizations jumped into petition politics. They dispatched telegrams to the Joint Select Committee and sent Herabai Tata and her daughter Mithan to England. In England, they gained new mentors. In addition to Annie Besant, Dorothy Jinarajadasa and Margaret Cousins, all members of the Theosophical Society who had been living in India and were involved with the women's movement, Millicent Fawcett, President of the National Union of Women's Suffrage Societies in England, and the American Carrie Chapman Catt, President of the International Suffrage Alliance, stepped forward to guide their efforts.

The petitions and telegrams sent to London claimed for women the same privileges accorded men. In other words, women with "the same qualifications as are laid down for men in any part of the Scheme" should be given the vote.[7] Herabai and Mithan pointed to women's role in social reform, the injustice of excluding them, and the importance of bringing India in line with the rest of the civilized world. Although their constituency was educated and had activist women like themselves, they argued that uneducated women and *pardanashin* [women who observed purdah] also wanted social change.

Meanwhile, Annie Besant, who had gone with Sarojini Naidu as a delegate to the Franchise Committee, played the "culture card." If the British continued to exclude women, she prophesied women would join political protests. The next step might be police intervention and if that happened, and the police touched these women, all hell would break loose. Indian men, she warned "would not tolerate police interference where women are concerned."[8]

It is interesting to note the differences in the arguments made to different audiences. In India, proponents of women's franchise located women in the home and asserted that their knowledge of domestic issues mandated political participation. In England, Indian women and their British allies led with the women's rights thesis and trumped with the culture card. In this environment, where special electorates and reserved seats were common and popular ways of addressing difference (of Muslims, Christians, landlords, the British, etc.), the ideology of gender as immutable seemed perfect to justify reservations and special provisions for yet another group. But the struggle at this time was for the simplest kind of participation—the vote. Special measures to ensure women's political participation were far beyond the vision of the proponents or the opposition.

In the end, Lord Montagu decided not to recommend female franchise in the face of conservative opposition. The House of Commons followed his lead but allowed provincial legislative councils to add women to the list of registered voters.[9] Women's organizations now worked in the provinces for the removal of sex disqualification and between 1920 and 1930, propertied women won the right to vote.[10] However, this was only one hurdle as women were still disqualified from membership in the legislatures. After the Women's Indian Association lobbied and met with members of the Muddiman Committee, the Governor General in quite another matter, Muthulakshmi warned, when women begin to challenge men for "places of honour and emoluments," the outcome will be "a fight between the sexes."[24]

Sarojini Naidu, Begum Shah Nawaz, and Mrs. Subbarayan represented women at the Second Round Table Conference. By this time Begum Shah Nawaz had undergone a change of heart and joined Naidu in demanding universal adult franchise.[25] Muthulakshmi Reddi and others who had supported reservations also changed their tune. Only Radhabai Subbarayan withstood pressure from friends and continued her support for reserved seats.[26] At the end of the conference, another committee, under Lord Lothian, was sent to India to collect evidence and opinions.

The Lothian Committee received documents from women supporting universal franchise, but they also heard from women who favored reservations.[27] These women were educated, articulate, and experienced activists. In terms of class background and commitment to social change, they were not unlike their sisters in the major organizations who opposed reservations and special measures to enfranchise more women. A good example is Mrs. Kumudini Basu, a graduate of Calcutta University and secretary of the Bharat Stree Mahamandal who proposed increasing the number of women voting by enfranchising educated women, and wives and widows over the age of 35. She believed non-communal reservations, for a fixed number of years, would lead the public to accept women legislators. But she expressed a concern that disturbed her peers, that is, the fear that the act of voting might force respectable women to mix with, and perhaps be confused with, "undesirable" women. Mrs. Basu's solution was to revive the cantonment laws, register prostitutes with the police, and use these lists to force them to use separate polling booths.[28] Other women presented similar schemes to increase women's political presence, always claiming to speak for large numbers of women like themselves.[29] When Mrs. Salita Mukherji explained reservations, she made it clear the places were for "women's women," individuals recommended by women's organizations that had existed for more than 10 years.[30] These views were replicated in other provinces. When reservations were discussed, Hindu women generally

1917), the National Council of Women in India [NCWI] (begun in 1925), and the All India Women's Conference [AIWC] (formed in 1927), had been established. During this time, Gandhi continued to speak to women's groups about constructive work.[15] Although the women's organizations were officially apolitical, many of their leaders were devoted to Gandhi and found his faith in women compelling. At the same time, they had difficulty complying with his request that they subordinate women's issues "to the anti-imperialist cause."[16]

The WIA was at first willing to cooperate with the Simon Commission; they wanted two women added to the list of members. This all changed after Congress convened an All-Parties Conference and issued the Nehru Report demanding dominion status and responsible government. This document insisted on universal adult franchise and joint electorates, and promised women "equal rights." The Women's Indian Association and the All India Women's Conference voted to join with Congress in boycotting the Simon Commission. But there were other educated women, acting without the imprimatur of the major organizations, who met with the commission and suggested giving the vote to literate women or reserving seats.[17] Gandhi further complicated the situation by demanding a promise of dominion status and, when the British refused, launching the Civil Disobedience movement.

This movement was in full swing when the Indian Statutory Commission submitted its report. It rejected adult franchise but supported a set of schemes to increase female franchise by extending the vote to wives and widows of property owners and literate women.[18] The commission considered, and rejected, reserved seats for women. It would have been difficult to implement, since the British were already committed to communal reservations, but they did not reject it for these reasons. Instead they argued it was not in the best interests of Indian women or representative institutions in India.[19]

Members of the commission expressed optimism about women's progress. Calling the changes in women's position made since the Montagu-Chelmsford Report "astounding," they attributed these advancements to the women's movement and congratulated its leaders. The goal was to get a few women into office; accordingly, they suggested special provisions so provincial Governors could nominate reformist women to the legislatures.[20] That their view of women was not unlike Naidu's, when she spoke to the Indian National Congress, becomes clear when one examines the quote, from an "Indian lady," they chose to include. She said,

The innate intelligence of the Indian woman, her feeling of domestic responsibility, her experience of household management, make her shrewd, penetrating, wise within her own sphere. . . . as the power passes more and more from the hands of the few to the hands of the many, more and more is the steadying influence of woman needed as the guardian of family life, not only inside but outside the family circle.[21]

But organized Indian women stood firm with Congress and boycotted the Round Table Conference that began in November of 1930. Nevertheless, the two Indian women who were nominated, Begum Jahan Ara Shah Nawaz and Mrs. Radhabai Subbarayan, both active in women's organizations, agreed to attend. This was the first time the issue of reservations was raised. At the conference, Shah Nawaz and Subbarayan recommended that five percent of seats be reserved for women as a way of introducing this concept to the general public.[22] Opposing them, the WIA, AIWC and NWCI issued a joint memorandum reiterating women's support for universal adult franchise. Behind the scenes they moved to discipline their members to only advocate "equality and no privileges" and "a fair field and no favor."[23]

When Gandhi signed the Gandhi-Irwin Pact and agreed to call off Civil Disobedience, planning for the Second Round Table Conference began. Now members of the women's organizations were eager to attend and cracks began to appear in their united front. The WIA continued to reject schemes such as the wifehood qualification to increase the number of women voters, but spoke in favor of reservations. Muthulakshmi Reddi denied women wanted special favors, but called reservations a *necessity* [italics mine]. She cautioned against placing too much faith in male gratitude. Yes, men had praised women's activism, but these accolades came when women were carrying out "men's mandate." Politics was

Council decided provincial legislatures could vote to admit women.[11] Although nine of eleven provinces voted to allow women to become members of the councils, no woman candidate was ever elected. Instead, women were nominated and this is how Dr. Muthulakshmi Reddi became the first Indian woman legislator.[12] At the time, Muthulakshmi protested that she was "neither a politician nor was I interested in politics except what directly concerned women's life."[13] In asking for the vote, women employed the discourse of "rights" as well as an essentialist discourse that women could play a special and unique role in Indian politics. Yet they asked for it not as a special interest group, which for all intents and purposes they seemed to be, but on the same terms as men—property. In practice, the only political power they gained was through nomination.

MOHANDAS KARAMCHAND GANDHI

By the late 1920s, Gandhi was an important influence on the women's movement. He returned from South Africa in 1915 and immediately began to court activist women. His non-cooperation movement, with its emphasis on boycotts and *swadeshi*, promised new roles for women. Bombay women were the first to mobilize, demonstrating against the Prince of Wales' visit. Before long, Congress leader C.R. Das' wife, sister, and niece were arrested selling khaddar in the streets of Calcutta. These were the actions Gandhi applauded; he objected to women petitioning the British government for the franchise. He urged them to abandon the vote, and instead, win equality by "working in complete accord and cooperation with their men and assisting them in every possible manner."[14]

THE SECOND DEMAND FOR FRANCHISE

In the years between the suspension of non-cooperation in 1922 and the appointment of the Simon Commission in 1927, to study the situation for the next India Act, three national women's organizations, the Women's Indian Association [WIA] (formed in argued against communal reservations, Muslim women for them. Behind the scenes, British feminists were lobbying Lord Lothian's committee and advising Indian women. Their activity involved contacting members of parliament to express their opinions, and giving Indian women advice on rhetoric and tactics. Mrs. Subbarayan, at this time appointed a member of the Lothian Committee, was a close friend of Eleanor Rathbone, a member of the House of Commons. In her letters to Subbarayan and other Indian women leaders, Rathbone urged them to accept any scheme that would increase women's presence. Their work hit the mark. In their final report, the Lothian Committee recommended various schemes for enfranchising more women: lowered property qualifications, wifehood if the husband met the 1919 property qualification, and literacy. They also endorsed reservations for the provincial legislatures. However, women would vote with their communities and therefore be voting and acting as Muslim women, Sikh women, women from the depressed classes.[31]

When Gandhi agreed to the Poona Pact, accepting reserved seats but not separate electorates for the depressed castes, he tacitly agreed to the Communal Award. The next step toward the India Act, the White Paper of 1933, repeated the *mantra* about the importance of women to Indian uplift but took two steps back from the recommendations of the Lothian Committee. In terms of the franchise, the White Paper endorsed women voting with their communities but placed restrictions on the wifehood qualification and eliminated the literacy qualification. However, they agreed with the concept of communal reservations for women.

Once again, the three women's organizations objected but this time their decision to publish a joint memorandum, reiterating the demand for adult franchise, produced dissension within their ranks. The leaders of the women's organizations objected to reservations, indirect election of women to the Federal Assembly, the wifehood qualification, separate electorates, and the Communal Award. First and foremost among the dissenters were Muslim women. For example, Begum Shah Nawaz supported communal electorates. She agreed with universal franchise but argued it would be impossible for Muslim women to campaign freely amongst a mixed electorate, they would only be comfortable talking to Muslim men and women.[32] Other women disagreed because they believed women needed to be voters and legislators to push a social reform agenda. Sushama Sen, a long standing member of the AIWC in Bihar, wrote that she and others in the Bihar branch "felt that education and the women's social impediments should be got over first before asking for Adult Franchise." Sen noted that some of the older women's organizations, for example, the Mahila Samiti and Aghore Nari Samiti of Calcutta and the Bihar Council of Women, did not support a rigid stance on universal franchise. While they wanted the electorate expanded by various means, they opposed reserved seats and separate electorates.[33]

Amrit Kaur, Muthulakshmi Reddi and Mrs. Hamid Ali (a Muslim who opposed the Communal Award) went to London to present the position of the women's organizations to the Joint Select Committee. Begum Shah Nawaz also attended, but as a member of the Indian delegation. Now women were speaking at the center of power with more than one voice. Kaur, Reddi, and Hamid Ali claimed they represented all Indian women, reiterated their support for universal franchise, but as a temporary and short-term measure agreed to accept the enfranchisement of literate and urban women.[34] Meanwhile, memoranda supporting schemes to enfranchise more women, and in some cases reservations, arrived from Sushama Sen and others. These views were also endorsed in petitions signed by hundreds of women.

The 1935 Government of India Act introduced reservations and complex methods of increasing the percentage of women voters: wives could vote in some provinces, literate women in others, and the wives of military officers in still others, always voting as members of their communities.[35] Although the number of women voters was significantly larger, women's organizations had a difficult time getting women to register and run for election. To make matters worse, Congress was reluctant to support women candidates for general seats. Nevertheless, women in the three major organizations worked hard to register women, field women candidates, and get out the vote.

When the elections were over, women held 56 of the 1,500 seats in the provincial legislatures: 41 had been returned from reserved constituencies, 10 from general constituencies, and five were nominated.[36] An additional 30 women were elected to the Central Assembly and a number of prominent women, among them Vijayalakshmi Pandit and Begum Shah Nawaz, gained prestigious positions. Hailing this as a victory for women's cause, the women's organizations continued to claim women were the only ones qualified to solve the problems of women and children.[37]

CONCLUSIONS

In the years following independence, members of the women's organizations felt betrayed by their male allies. They did not receive the rewards they expected, especially nomination to influential positions and support for the reform of Hindu family law. Nevertheless, they stayed loyal to the concept of universal franchise with no special privileges for women. Women members of the Constituent Assembly, opposed special concessions for women and so reservations disappeared with universal franchise. Mary John has commented on how minority and communal rights were counterpoised to women's rights. In the end, religious and minority rights were perceived as working against social reforms that would benefit women. This ideology continued to dominate the women's movement through the early 1970s when the Committee on the Status of Women in India rejected reservations. This document warned that reservations would "narrow their [women's] outlook," "precipitate similar demands from various other interests and communities and threaten national integration," perpetuate women's "unequal status."[38] Vina Mazumdar and Lotika Sarkar's note of dissent was the first document in post-independence India to suggest reservations for women could have positive consequences.[39]

Through the 1920s and 1930s, there were three positions on women's role in politics. Leaders of the women's organizations believed women should be heard because they understood the special needs of women and children. British feminists, who by the twentieth century had made Indian women's issues a cornerstone of their platform, insisted political participation was the "right" of Indian women and would lead to social reform. Despite their critique of imperial politics, the majority of these women believed that British rule was benevolent and ultimately beneficial for their Indian sisters. Gandhi insisted that "rights," in the western sense, were of no value to Indian women and warned this movement diverted valuable resources from the fight for freedom. He urged women to join political protests and work with their less fortunate sisters, and above all to trust that leaders, like himself, would not tolerate a political system unfair to women.[40]

In the first movement to gain the vote, Indian women agreed on the goal but presented different arguments to different audiences. In India, they asked for the franchise to bring their special knowledge to the political process and, in England, because it was their "right." Since there was no discussion of universal franchise at this time, the debate revolved around questions of male support, women's fitness for this responsibility, and whether or not women wanted the vote.

The second movement, lasting from the Simon Commission to the India Act of 1935, aimed at giving women a greater presence in politics so they could work for social reform and the nation's uplift. By this time Gandhi had an extraordinary following among women and he had little faith in petition politics and even less in franchise as a solution for women's problems. Leaders of the women's movement were not ready to relinquish petition politics but wholeheartedly supported the Congress demand for universal franchise and equal (not communal) representation.

During the drawn-out debate and discussions over the India Act, women's organizations clung to the idea of universal franchise far longer than Congress and far longer than was politically expedient. Although they ultimately accepted various schemes to increase the number of women voting and for reservations, they did so reluctantly, and continued to praise universal franchise. Women participated in the elections of 1937 and found reservations served them well. They were well aware that few women were ready for the rough and tumble of politics, and that political parties were not committed to supporting them as candidates. Yet when they had the opportunity to voice their opinion on reservations, at the Constituent Assembly, women sided with men against their continuance. Since reservations had benefited them, their ready dismissal of guaranteed representation seems an anomaly.

Mary John argues women's hostility to reservations stems from the fact reservations have been designed to right historical wrongs, not address present inequalities. Consequently, they are viewed as "inimical to the national interest."[41] This may explain the vote of women in 1949 and their rejection of reservations until the 1970s, but it does not address their earlier opposition.

I believe women's intense dislike of reservations derived from their view of women's role in politics. Sarojini Naidu's assertion, that women belonged in politics because the nation needed their special talents and experience as nurturers, became the dominant ideology among Muslim women and Hindu women, those who supported reservations, and those who opposed them. Rooted in the nineteenth century ideology of the "new woman," by the twentieth century this concept had been accepted and transformed by women. It was an ideal construct: it justified women's entry into public life, confirmed the work of their organizations, and rejected gender competition. But this argument also includes a litmus test for women in politics: was their political work beneficial to women?

Muthulakshmi Reddi came to what she called "the painful conclusion" that just having a woman in a powerful position was not the answer. She would far rather see, she wrote, "one or two good women . . . in each council or assembly to represent women's point of view." Appalled by the appointment of undeserving women, she concluded, "*Women are still new to the public work here and unless we have chosen women of character, grit, and courage to occupy places of honour and responsibility, women cannot help to achieve much*"[42] [italics mine]. She was not alone in expressing these sentiments; the records of the women's organizations are full of memos about the importance of having the right kind of woman in office.

What was the "right kind" of woman? She had to be educated, at least middle-class, a wife and mother, and interested in the problems of women. From the time women were first allowed to vote, respectable women expressed their horror that prostitutes, when property owners, were enfranchised. When women's organizations claimed they spoke for all women they did not include prostitutes in their definition of women. At times, they claimed to speak for the wives of landlords and *pardanashin* and claimed these women wanted progressive legislation. However, they later opposed extending the franchise to the wives of property owners who they said would vote with their husbands and double the conservative voice. Those who disagreed with the major women's organizations and supported reservations and increasing the female franchise, insisted on complex schemes to ensure that only women like themselves would be represented. In the end, neither opponents nor proponents of reservations were interested in bringing women unlike themselves into politics.

Opposition to and support for reservations were based on a construction of woman that was narrow and class-based. By the 1930s, the major women's organizations claimed to speak for all Indian women and never doubted their right to do so. Faced with dissension over the Communal Award, or over extending the franchise and reservations, they quashed minority views and presented a united front. Although they adamantly opposed special concessions, reservations, and separate electorates, all three became a reality. And their opposition, tied as it was to an ideal vision of "sisters under the sari," and loyalty to Gandhi, became the reigning ideology of the women's movement. Looking back at this period, I am disappointed at the absence of democratic impulses in the women's movement. Certainly there were exceptions, and I would cite Saraladevi Chaudhurani, as well as women who joined the Marxists, who had a more radical view of women's role in politics, but the majority of women leaders accepted the patriarchal position that politics were men's domain and women's role was to humanize/feminize that domain. Both reservationists and anti-reservations wanted the "right" kind of woman in politics. Neither group wanted women of all classes, castes, and religions to answer the question "what do women want?" for fear the answers would not be the same as theirs.

Medicine

Managing Midwifery in India[1]

THE PROBLEM

In 1934 the All-India Women's Conference [AIWC] passed a resolution at its annual meeting calling for legislation requiring the "compulsory registration" of all *dhais* and midwives.[2] The AIWC, inaugurated in 1927, was fast emerging as India's premier women's organization, with branches all over the country and a membership in the thousands. By this act, reformist middle-class Indian women made it clear that they agreed with Western missionaries, medical personnel, and British authorities that traditional Indian birth attendants [*dhais*] had to be replaced by midwives trained in Western medicine and hygiene. Their resolution reflected a widely shared perception of the *dhai*, expressed by Dr. Miss Jerbanoo E. Mistry, LMS, to the Bombay Presidency Women's Council several years earlier:

The *dhai* considers herself qualified to attend all labours normal and abnormal, and all the pelvic diseases. Cleanliness is a thing unknown to her. Soap and water are her great enemies. Often she is so dirty she stinks, and her hands and nails are covered with dirt, particularly the nails which are long and perfectly black on account of dirt underneath. To ask her to wash her hands before making an examination is to inflict on her a great unforgivable indignity.[3]

By the 1930s, educated middle-class Indian women, regarded as the legitimate spokespersons on issues of concern to their gender, supported Western medicine over indigenous medical systems and advocated government control over traditional practitioners. In taking this position, these "new women" were making it clear that they stood with the progressive elements of society against age-old customs entwined with religion and superstition. At the same time, they were taking a stand against their lower-caste and less fortunate sisters, the *dhais*, who depended on this work to earn their livelihood.

David Arnold has asserted that the widespread promotion of Western medicine and public-health projects advanced the security of the colonial state in India. Part of this agenda necessitated the displacement or subordination of indigenous medical systems and practitioners, which represented "rival systems of ideas and authority." "In this sense," writes Arnold, "imperial hegemony stood for a deliberate confrontation with indigenous values and political power."[4]

But the British rulers were not particularly interested in the health of their colonial subjects, and neither British nor Indian men were concerned with the process of birthing. It was women missionaries and the wives of Indian officials who brought these issues into the public arena. When they did so, they found allies among the newly emerging class of Western-educated Indians. Gradually the wholesale acceptance of Western-style birthing practices, regarded as rational and scientific, became part and parcel of progressive Indian society. These ideas were given life in the magazines and journals of the day, which contained articles on "scientific" birth practices and congratulated medical graduates. New medical institutions for women appeared: lying-in hospitals, nursing homes, new female wards in older hospitals, and institutions specifically designed to train female doctors and nurses. Women's organizations, representing the "new women," took up the issues of high maternal and infant mortality rates. The colonial government rewarded with titles those wealthy and influential Indians who sponsored medical institutions, and gave handsome salaries to the new medical graduates. And the *dhai*, a living reminder of the failure to realize that dream completely, was soundly denounced for her ignorance and failure to change.

In the mid-nineteenth century the *dhai* had seemed the appropriate person to assist in childbirth. She was, however, gradually transformed, in the literature generated by the British and progressive Indians, into a wizened hag, responsible for India's high maternal and infant mortality rate. This transformation of the *dhai* into the evil witch of progressive India raises a number of issues: how did this transformation take place, how were the issues framed to suit the needs of the British rulers, and how were these ideas transferred to and then expressed by Indians? And finally, what were the consequences for the *dhais* and their clients?

OBSTETRICS IN PRE-BRITISH INDIA

As D. N. Kakar and many others have pointed out, every community has "cultural guidelines" for its medical system and uses these guidelines to define problems requiring medical assistance, the experts who deliver treatment, and family members with ultimate authority over treatment.[5] Ayurveda, the oldest medical system in India derived from the Vedas, contained no section on obstetrics or gynecology. However, these topics were discussed at some length in the *samhitas* [Vedic texts] of Charaka and Susruta. Their writings, a combination of practical physiological advice, theology, and ritual, also include a discussion of healthy parents, fetal development, labor, and the management of the post-delivery period. It is clear that the professional in charge was the midwife,[6] whom Dr. Julius Jolly has characterized as an "experienced and courageous women of advanced age and with clean clothes before whom she [the birthing mother] may not feel shy, who have cut their nails and who cheer her with friendly words."[7]

Charles Leslie has convincingly argued that the introduction of Unani [Greek] medicine to India resulted in a syncretic system.[8] The paramount concern was the health of the prospective parents and the regimen to be followed by the pregnant woman during labor and the post-partum period. The designated birth attendants continued to be experienced women and midwives. Pregnancy and birthing were seen as natural processes. When difficulties occurred they were seen as the result of the mother's physiological problems, failure to follow the rituals designed for her pregnancy, or because the fetus had not been properly formed.[9] The medical texts cataloged these problems and suggested remedies that could be carried out, during or following delivery, by an experienced woman.[10] Dr. John Fryer, who visited India at the end of the seventeenth century and had some knowledge of women in the most prestigious zenanas as well as peasant women, wrote that women were "quick in Labour."[11] And there are other travelers' and medical accounts that suggest giving birth in India was no more hazardous than it was in England.[12]

EUROPEAN MEDICINE IN INDIA

When European medicine was first introduced to India it encountered syncretic systems developed from an interchange of ideas between Ayurvedic and Unani medicine. Male practitioners of Ayurvedic and Unani medicine (systems closed to women because transmission was through the "sacred" languages, Sanskrit and Arabic) had not replaced women as traditional birth attendants.

In the first three decades of the nineteenth century, colonial rulers tolerated and sometimes patronized indigenous learning. As a consequence, Ayurvedic and Unani medicine were taught alongside Western medicine in Sanskrit College. But in 1835 these courses were dropped when the government decided to "make European medicine the only acknowledged system of study."[13] In fact, Lord Macaulay marked this victory by ordering a cannon salute of 50 rounds when an Indian medical student performed his first dissection of a human body.[14]

However, the British were not at this time concerned with extending the benefits of Western medicine to the entire Indian population. Roger Jeffery, in *The Politics of Health in India*, has pointed out that imperialism worked against indigenous healing traditions by depriving practitioners of elite patronage.[15] The Indian Medical Service was designed to serve only the Indian Civil Service and the army; that others derived benefit was more accident than policy.

The British at this time were articulating a version of gender relations that provided justification for continued rule. James Mill, in his influential *History of British India* (first published in 1826), argued that women's position could be used as an indicator of society's advancement. He declared that no society could advance, and here he was particularly commenting on Hindus, until women were allowed to associate on equal terms with men.[16] Mill and his contemporaries were particularly struck by sex-segregation in India. Unable to comprehend, let alone enter, the zenana, they concluded that separation meant oppression and expressed the hope that the British model of gender roles and gender relations would be emulated in India.

These early British critics of Hindu and Muslim treatment of women paid no attention to the topic of medical care for women. Rather, it was sati, enforced widowhood, and early marriage that engaged their attention. Anxiety about the health of the army, not Indian women, led to compulsory medical examinations for prostitutes.[17] They cared about European troops and European quarters and initiated sanitary measures designed to control "native" women.[18]

THE INDIAN SITUATION IN THE MID-NINETEENTH CENTURY

Our knowledge of the day-to-day practice of midwifery in mid-nineteenth century India is limited by scanty evidence and obfuscated by polemics. In Lal Behari Day's essay on peasant life in Bengal, written in 1872, the midwife emerges as a kindly and familiar figure in the village. Having narrated the birth of a child in the home of Badan, a Bengali peasant, Day wrote:

Rupa's mother—for she was the village midwife—was in all her glory. From the door of the lying-in room, into which no one, not even the father of the newly-born child, might enter—for it is regarded as ceremoniously unclean—she was every now and then showing the baby with evident pride and satisfaction, as if the newcomer were her own son or grandson.[19]

In wealthier families, giving birth was undoubtedly carried out with greater attention to norms of seclusion. Since the upwardly mobile families of Bengal emulated the Muslim custom of purdah, women from the higher castes/classes generally stayed inside the home. A special space or room within the women's quarters was set aside for childbirth and only the birthing mother and midwife were allowed inside. Because birthing was considered ritually impure, the mother and newborn child were regarded as highly susceptible to both diseases and evil spirits. Consequently, the room was not ventilated and items of clothing and bedding were not cleaned until a required number of days had passed.[20] But customs varied throughout India and the poorer classes were unable to observe either a long period of confinement or the attendant rituals. While some authors have suggested that this may have been to the advantage of these women, poverty obviously brought other hardships.

Among some members of the Calcutta elite, especially the highly Westernized members of the Brahmo Samaj and those influenced by them, advances in midwifery were readily adopted. Meredith Borthwick has commented on the eagerness of the *bhadralok* [respectable middle-class] to "use the new medical knowledge." As early as 1848 the report of the Midwifery Hospital of Calcutta Medical College proudly announced that their graduates regularly attended confinements and that "respectable Natives" had abandoned the custom of secluding the new mother and her baby in an unventilated, filthy outhouse or side room. Although Borthwick doubts the adoption of European medical practices had advanced so quickly, she presented convincing evidence that the Brahmos and their circle read Western medical treatises on midwifery, wrote comments on these texts, and put many of the new ideas into practice. She suggests that a large percentage of the urban middle class were reading articles about Western medicine in the Brahmo magazines and gradually adopting new ideas about medical care, hygiene, and midwifery.[21]

Lal Behari Day portrayed a pleasant and well-meaning midwife. In contrast, S.C. Bose, author of *The Hindoos as they Are: A Description of the Manners, Customs and Inner Life of Hindoo Society in Bengal* (written in 1881 and quoted extensively in Borthwick), focused on the ignorance of the low-caste *dhai* and the filthy conditions of the birthing room.[22] This should come as no surprise since most of the earliest treatises aimed at improving conditions were translations of English works (for example, Shib Chunder Deb's *Shishupalan*, 1857, was adapted from Andre Combe's *Treatise on the Physiological and Moral Management of Infancy*) and attacked the traditional way of giving birth as well as traditional caregivers.[23]

ENTER MISSIONARIES, MEMSAHIBS AND VICEROYS' WIVES

Indian birth practices were of little interest to colonial authorities until missionary women made them an issue. A few single women arrived to begin girls' schools in the early decades of the nineteenth century, but by and large women missionaries were wives whose job was to help their husbands by teaching the wives and children of male converts. In the period following the rebellion of 1857 the number of single women missionaries increased significantly. More Indian men were willing to have their wives and daughters taught by women missionaries and England was experiencing a "surplus" of unmarried, educated women. It was in the 1860s that a number of missionary societies sponsored separate women's associations. Designed to recruit, train, and support female missionaries, these associations focused on education in the zenana.[24] These women, proto-feminists of a particularly virulent Christian variety, gained entrance to the inner compartments where they did some teaching and a great deal of observing. According to Balfour and Young, the impetus for the very first *dhai* training schemes derived from the efforts of missionary women who taught in the zenanas and witnessed their young pupils dying in childbirth.[25]

As early as 1869 Miss Clara Swain, MD, a member of the Women's Foreign Missionary Society of the Methodist Episcopal Church (USA) arrived in India. A decade later the Church of England Zenana Missionary Society sent out Miss Fanny Butler, MD.[26] The missionary societies that sponsored these women all published magazines that helped make women in England and America aware of conditions in India. By the 1880s, educated men and women who supported mission activities believed education and Western medicine would better the condition of women in India.

Further efforts to improve medical care for women were begun by the wives of viceroys and later supported by the government.[27] Missionary records assert that the efforts of Lady Harriet Dufferin, wife of the Indian Viceroy Lord Dufferin (1884–1888), were a consequence of the work of Miss Beilby. Miss Beilby came to Lucknow as a medical missionary in 1875. While she was there, the Maharaja of Punna, a native state in Bundelcund, asked her to come and attend his wife. The Maharani recovered and told Miss Beilby, "I want you to tell the Queen and the Prince and Princess of Wales and the men and women of England, what the women of India suffer when they are sick." Returning to England, Miss Beilby had an audience with Queen Victoria, who reportedly said, "We had no idea it was as bad as this. Something must be done for the poor creatures. We wish it generally known that we sympathize with every effort to relieve the suffering of the women of India." When Lady Dufferin was leaving for India in 1883, the Queen instructed her to initiate some plan for providing medical aid to the women of India. After completing a study of the situation, writing to the wives of governors to elicit their support, and enlisting the sympathy of the Raja of Rutlam, Lady Harriet was ready to launch her scheme.[28] The Countess of Dufferin's Fund, begun in 1885, is generally treated as the starting point for a history of Western medical care for Indian women. This was certainly not the first training scheme for medical women in India but it was the first coordinated program with official support.

The Dufferin Fund, or, more correctly, the National Association for Supplying Female Medical Aid to the Women of India, stated its aims as: providing medical tuition to doctors, hospital assistants, nurses and midwives; medical relief through dispensaries, female wards, female doctors and female hospitals; and training nurses and midwives. The Fund was administered by a central committee that included members of the Viceroy's Council and Home Department, and other influential Englishmen, as well as titled Indians such as the Maharaja Sir Jotendro Mohun Tagore, Sir Syed

Ahmed Khan, and Sir Dinshaw Manockjee Petit. Indians participated in this scheme by serving on the boards of local branches, donating money, and constructing buildings. The lists of board members of the various branches and of donors to the Fund read like a Who's Who of famous and titled Indians. In return, donations to the favorite schemes of the viceroy's wife were rewarded with favors and titles. This led one critic to complain that there were too many patrons constructing hospitals without any thought for operating costs and staffing. These new monuments to modern medicine were powerful symbols that there were many among the "chiefs and princes" who shared the colonial view of science and the welfare of women.[29]

The Duff Fund first worked to secure more women doctors to serve the women of India. Scholarships were set up to train Indian women in England, and for English and European women who would promise to practice in India. Those who graduated were guaranteed handsome salaries: over 2000 rupees per year with a horse and house allowance of approximately 400 rupees per year for a woman doctor, and at least 400 rupees per year for a trained midwife.[30]

As wives of succeeding viceroys established a host of schemes to bring medical care ("relief" in their terms) to Indian women, they found allies among Indian men who were either convinced that Western medical care was valuable and beneficial, or saw support of these schemes as a route to honor and decoration, or both. Their other allies were English men and women anxious to claim a civilizing mission for the colonial presence in India; English women seeking professional careers and opportunities for flexing their new feminist muscles; and Indian women, the products of the new schools and colleges for women, who also sought professional training.

One of the main aims of the Dufferin Fund was to train Indian women. The Countess of Dufferin was particularly concerned with the training of *dhais* and envisaged a time when it would be illegal for Indian midwives to practice without a license.[31] English writings about day-to-day life in India supported the work of the Fund. Reporting on medical care in India, the journalist Mary Frances Billington (a writer for *The Daily Graphic* who visited India in the 1890s and wrote 28 articles on women's lives) commented:

That infant mortality is very high, is not on account of evil intent, but is due to the appalling ignorance of the *dhais*, the professional class of midwives or monthly nurses whose methods of treatment are simply barbarous, and, indeed, viewed in the light of our scientific knowledge, seem as if they would be enough to kill every unfortunate victim upon whom they practiced.[32]

Other vicereines followed the model set by the Countess of Dufferin. In 1903 Lady Curzon set up a special fund to train midwives and by 1916 the Lady Hardinge Medical College for women was opened in Delhi.

WESTERN MEDICINE AND INDIAN MODERNIZERS

These efforts to extend Western medical care facilities and personnel to Indian women were very popular among Indians who considered themselves modernizers. The enlightened among the elite served on medical boards, donated money to hospitals, and refuted those who argued that Indian women were not ready to take advantage of these new facilities. When Maulvi Qamar-uddin said at a meeting at Gaya on 20 December 1889 that many Indian women would not accept a European woman doctor, Maulvi Dilawar Hussain Ahmad denied this was true:

I have no doubt . . . that all the women of this district, especially of the higher classes, will hail the coming of a Lady Doctor as a special boon . . . My own opinion is that the death of many a lady of our country must be ascribed to the disinclination to engage the services of a Doctor of the other sex . . .[33]

Although the Dufferin Fund was a private organization, its unofficial connections with government made it extremely influential.

Meanwhile, the central committee of the association strengthened the semi-official nature of their mission by securing government inspection of their hospitals. Practically, this meant that women's hospitals, and the medical women running them, were under the authority of the Civil Surgeon.

The first Indian women to complete degrees in medicine were marginal in their own societies. Kadambini Basu, a graduate of Bethune College of Calcutta University in 1882, was one of India's first women to receive a BA. She entered medical college in 1883 and soon after married her long-time mentor and friend Dwarkanath Ganguli, an advocate of male-female equality. When the government in 1884 announced a scholarship of 20 rupees a month for women medical students, Kadambini took advantage of this assistance and in 1886 was awarded the GBMC [Graduate of Bengal Medical College]. Kadambini immediately began a private practice and found her services much in demand. By 1888 she was appointed to the Lady Dufferin Women's Hospital with a monthly salary of 300 rupees.[34]

Other Indian women who sought medical degrees were either from reformist religious families, like Kadambini, members of families who were converts to Christianity, or rebels against tradition. Anandabai Joshi (born in 1865) belongs to this last category. From childhood she had pursued her lessons with determination, and she continued to do so (she had married her tutor) after marriage. At the age of 13 she bore and lost a son, and it was this experience, so her biographer informs us, that made her decide to become a medical doctor.[35] Seeking financial help for her education, her husband wrote a letter which appeared in *The Missionary Review*, published from Princeton, New Jersey. Before long, Anandabai received an invitation to study in America with promises of support. Every community criticized her for wanting to leave India to study medicine abroad. Christian missionaries opposed her leaving without baptism and Brahmins denounced her plans. Crowds dogged her every move and surrounded the post-office building in which she and her husband lived, threatening his ability to function as postmaster. Finally, Anandabai decided to address the people of Serampore in the Baptist College Hall. In this brave speech, she recounted the public harassment she faced in the streets, reiterated her desire to remain an orthodox Hindu, and asked her co-religionists not to excommunicate her. A person's duty to herself, she boldly argued, was more important than conventional gender roles.[36] Anandabai proceeded to the USA, studied, and graduated from the Women's Medical College in Philadelphia in 1884. Unfortunately, she died in 1886 without beginning her practice.

Another Indian woman who fits this category is Dr. Rukhmabai (1864–1951), who attended the London School of Medicine for Women and completed her education with an MD from Brussels. Rukhmabai had earlier caused a sensation when she refused to live with the man to whom she had been married as a child. Her husband demanded restitution of his conjugal rights and when Rukhmabai refused, she was threatened with imprisonment. When the case was finally over, she went to London to study medicine. Returning to India in 1895, she first became house surgeon at the Cama Hospital in Bombay and then took charge of the new hospital for women at Surat. She was among the first Indian women in the Women's Medical Service from which she retired in 1930.[37]

Dr. Hilda Lazarus was one of the first Indian Christians to qualify as a medical doctor. Her grandfathers, both from Brahmin families, had converted to Christianity and suffered the hostility of their communities long before Hilda was born. Born in Vizagapatnam (now in Andhra Pradesh) Hilda studied first in her father's school and then at a local college for her BA. She completed her BA at Presidency College, Madras, and received her MB and MS from Madras Medical College. Following graduation she was appointed assistant to the obstetrician and gynecologist at Lady Hardinge Medical College Hospital in 1917. As the first Indian woman appointed from London to the Women's Medical Service in India she was much in demand and within a few months was transferred and appointed resident medical officer of Dufferin Hospital in Calcutta. Dr. Lazarus spent 30 years in the Women's Medical Service, retiring in 1947 as the chief medical officer.[38]

These women and their colleagues who sought medical careers became part of the "new women's" network which encompassed professional women and women in the new social reform organizations. Most of these women were married to men whose careers marked them as "modern." But it was not just because of their careers or those of their husbands that they acknowledged the superiority of Western science. They were forging their own identities and in doing so were sorting out which aspects of tradition they wished to retain and which they wished to cast aside.

CONSTRUCTION OF THE DANGEROUS *DHAI*

Commenting on the work of women medical workers and health care in India in the 1920s, Margaret Balfour and Ruth Young, both British doctors, wrote that the "insoluble problem" was the "indigenous midwife, or *dhai* who has been presiding over childbirth for ages."[39] What had begun as concern expressed by missionaries over the medical services available for women who observed purdah, now had widespread support. The new middle class wanted Western medical knowledge and techniques. British officials expressed an interest in childbirth as they began to accept responsibility for public-health measures. At the same time, organized sectors of the economy—factories, mines and plantations—were impacted by new international standards that required the provision of some health care. Even the British rulers of India, who styled themselves a "civilizing influence," now had to explain the existence of high infant mortality rates.

Dyarchy, the name of power sharing outlined in the 1919 India Act, placed nation-building portfolios in the hands of Indian legislators. Transferred subjects at this time included local self-government, education, health, public works, agriculture and industry, while revenue and law and order remained in the hands of the governor. It was a time when the Indian population was increasing, the trade balance had shifted against India, and agricultural productivity was on the decline. At this very difficult period in history, middle-class Indians (the limited franchise made it possible for only a small percentage of the total population to vote) had become partners in the "civilizing mission." They too were now engaged in answering awkward questions about the health and welfare of the Indian population.

Details regarding the condition of the Indian working class were gathered through a number of studies, some commissioned by the government, others carried out by British and Indian organizations. Dagmar Curjel's report on women's labor in Bengal industries (1923) claimed that even though the Calcutta municipal authorities employed trained midwives to provide free services for industrial workers, women did not seek them out for treatment.[40] Whether they failed to utilize these services because of ignorance or custom

or because they could not afford the time away from work and/
or household-nurturing tasks, cannot be ascertained. British
observers generally reached the first conclusion, yet the records
indicate that women workers were not asked this question. The
Textile Factories Labour Committee, for example, examined only
three female workers; no other women gave evidence before this
committee. The Royal Commission on Labour in India, which
included one woman on the 12-person committee, made a serious
effort to speak with one or two women at each factory visited.
However, for substantial information about women they relied
mainly on middle-class Indian women who were themselves
health professionals and/or involved with women's organizations.
They came to the predictable conclusion that more women
doctors, trained midwives, medical clinics, and maternity benefits
were essential.[41]

In their report, the Commission (known as the Whitley
Commission) pointed out the great need for inspectresses in the
factories. Medically qualified inspectresses would be best, they
argued, because they could then supervise trained midwives and
even try to gain the confidence of the *dhais* working in the area
and attempt to raise the standard of their work. This report insisted
that the work of the traditional birth attendant had to be restricted
or maternity schemes would never succeed.[42] The writers of this
report were never clear why the maternity schemes, most of which
involved some payment for pre- and post-maternity leave, could
not work unless trained midwives were involved. However, one
can hypothesize that the issue at hand was social control. Employers
often refused to give women maternity benefits, arguing that
these women took the half-pay or whatever amount was set,
stayed away from their regular place of employment, and went to
work elsewhere.[43] Obviously, a trained midwife in the employ of
the factory could be used to report on their deviant behavior.

That social control was the issue gains further credence later
in this report when plantations are discussed. Plantation owners
willingly gave their female workers half-pay for a period before
and after the birth of a child as well as a lump-sum cash bonus.
Those who wrote the commission report suggested that the

employer also provide the services of a doctor and trained midwife, but recommended withhólding the bonus from the women unless these services were used. And they made it clear that this element of coercion (which they termed a "benefit") "would go far to overcome the prejudice in favour of the untrained *dhai*".[44]

Here we can only guess why the plantation owners were so solicitous of pregnant women when they generally treated their workforce so callously.[45] Probably they viewed reproduction as a less expensive method of labor recruitment than any other. Consequently they did not like *dhais*, who, according to Dr. Whitell, Civil Surgeon of Lakhimpur, operated as abortionists in towns outside the jurisdiction of the planters.[46] We do not know how often women workers made use of their services, but there is evidence women working in plantations did not want to give birth to children who would experience the same misery as their mothers.

The women's organizations, formed in the period after the First World War, focused on the *dhai* when they looked at high maternal and infant mortality rates. Partly this was due to their educational background and identification with a progressive ideology; partly it was a result of their close connections with activist British women. In addition, they received government grants when their goals matched Viceregal schemes to help women. [47]

It was in 1919 that Lady Chelmsford became interested in medical care for women and children and launched the All-India Maternity and Child Welfare League. Designed to co-ordinate activities that had begun during the war years, League branches trained midwives and women health visitors, founded maternity homes, and set up baby centers and crèches. Although initiated by English women, the association soon began to include Indian women.[48] And in 1924, Lady Reading began the "Baby Week" movement. In an effort to promote healthy infants, traveling exhibits including posters, literature, and "baby contests" appeared throughout India.

When one looks at the records of women's organizations it would appear that they followed the League's lead. While various organizations were begun in Bombay in the 1920s—for example, the Bombay Presidency Infant Welfare Society (1921) and the

Bombay Presidency Baby and Health Week Association (1924)—
these organizations remained under European control until the
1930s.[49] More representative of Indian women was the Bombay
Presidency Women's Council. Begun immediately following the
First World War in an effort to coordinate and give focus to various
groups formed during the war years, the Council was composed
of both British and Indian women's organizations. They supported
maternity benefits and urged industries to do more to improve
the working conditions of women.[50] But they saw the high infant
mortality rate in terms of inadequate medical care, not wages or
living conditions.[51] Factory owners took note of this organization,[52]
and by the 1930s were giving substantial donations to establish
medical centers and crèches in the areas adjacent to their factories.
The women, in turn, praised the factory owners for their interest
in women's welfare, and supported bills for the registration of
dhais and midwives.[53]

The National Council of Women in India was similarly involved
in schemes to encourage maternity benefits for women, develop
more medical centers, and open crèches for children. They also
called for additional schemes to train nurses and midwives and
thought that both should be registered. Recognizing the difficulties
involved in attracting the "right class" to this profession, they asked
the government to improve the conditions of work for nurses and
make special appeals to get "refined girls" to enter the profession.[54]

The All-India Women's Conference did not begin to comment
on medical issues until 1931. During the following years they
passed resolutions supporting maternity and child welfare acts,[55]
the appointment of medical women to positions where they could
advise the government on health policies,[56] instruction on birth
control,[57] and licensing midwives.[58] By the 1930s, the three all-
India women's organizations were determined to abolish *dhais*
and replace them with midwives trained in Western techniques.

Even social scientists who understood the relationship between
poverty and mortality, blamed indigenous medical systems and
practitioners for India's appalling statistics on maternal and infant
mortality. Anstey wrote in 1929:

The existence of indigenous medical systems and of indigenous medical practitioners militates against the adoption of Western methods and the problem of improving the health of women and children is complicated by the strength of the customs which make women backward in seeking medical attention from male doctors, even where such attention is available.[59]

By the mid-1930s most of the provincial governments had passed legislation to mandate the registration of nurses and midwives and appointed regulatory councils. In Madras they hoped this legislation would "eliminate the *dhai* altogether," but in Bombay it was designed to place the profession on a higher level.[60] In the Bombay debates, Mr. A.N. Surve of Bombay City North made the following statement about midwives:

But about midwives, the question is more serious. Midwives, if they are not trained, are a source of great danger to society at large. The infant mortality rate in urban areas is tremendous, simply because the *dhais* are allowed to officiate at the deliveries. The infant mortality rate in India was so high some years ago that the conscience of welfare workers was roused and I am glad to say that we have now made considerable progress in reducing the infant mortality by opening maternity homes and hospitals in urban areas. That has gone a long way in reducing infant mortality.[61]

TRAINING SCHEMES FOR *DHAIS* AND MIDWIVES

Despite demands that all midwives be trained and licensed, remarkably little seems to have been done to make this a reality. Missionary schemes begun in the nineteenth century, always small and limited in scope, gradually disappeared. The newer hospital programs turned out trained midwives in less than adequate numbers. These trained midwives were in great demand and upon graduation were immediately hired by hospitals, nursing homes, municipalities, and health centers. The first programs assumed *dhais* could be trained in Western techniques and technology of childbirth and fit into a European medical scheme. But traditional *dhais* resisted this training. According to those associated with the Dufferin Fund there were four reasons why midwives did not attend the lectures designed for their benefit. First, they regarded their time as money and wanted to be paid to attend. Second, they found the training schemes interfered with their ability to practice their craft. Third, they did not recognize the superiority of the Western way of childbirth. And finally, clients were satisfied with their services.[62] An earlier report of the Countess of Dufferin Fund noted it was difficult to find women who knew enough English for the midwife course,[63] but this reason was left out of later documents. Because of what they saw as the intransigence of traditional midwives, the Dufferin Fund decided to "create a class of nurses and midwives who, we might hope, would in time supplant the dhais, or, by successfully competing with them, force them to seek the instruction offered to them."[64]

Reformers argued that a great many lives would be saved if *dhais* learned the basic principles of hygiene, saw excessive bleeding as a danger signal rather than beneficial cleansing, and called for assistance in difficult cases. But the *dhais* were not willing to learn about Western medicine. As Balfour concluded in one of her studies, *dhais* would not attend lectures because they were "afraid of losing their work and reputation for doing so, [and so] they are trying, out of jealousy to create distrust of, and prejudice against, the European mode of confinement in the minds of ignorant women."[65] Even when they accepted training and "kits" containing soap, scissors, etc., it was difficult to provide further supervision. Some schemes involved follow-up visits by women doctors and rewards for successful deliveries but in other cases the precious kits were locked up for safekeeping. The best schemes were those associated with hospitals and sympathetic Indian women doctors.

It was clear that very few Europeans appreciated the number and variety of functions performed by the *dhai*. Knowledge of hygiene and the ability to recognize an abnormal birth did not change the basic and fundamental polluting nature of the birthing experience. Nor did they comprehend that "refined girls," especially if they were from the high castes, would be unwilling to serve women of lower rank or be involved in cleaning up the afterbirth, washing the infant, and providing post-partum care. To call the *dhai* a "traditional birth attendant" rather than a midwife would have been more accurate since she performed a variety of functions associated with the birth of a child.

Those women who were part of the medical system, women like Dr. Rukhmabai and Dr. Lazarus, sought to work within that system to improve schemes to train women. Both have been credited with developing successful plans to train *dhais*. Their programs have not received a great deal of attention; perhaps because they worked quietly and diligently through the hospitals they served. Both were knowledgeable about local conditions and sensitive to the problems that would arise if the training were directed by males, delivered in English, or in other ways unsuitable for the *dhais* or the clientele served.

CONCLUSIONS

An interesting account of the transition taking place in an urban middle-class family can be found in the memoirs of Shudha Mazumdar. Khirodai, a midwife "reputed to be good," attended her when she had her first child, in 1914. Shudha described this woman as having a kindly face, wearing a "spotless white sari," and being very knowledgeable about her work. Shudha's labor was difficult but she delivered a healthy child with the help of the midwife and two maidservants. The windows of the accouchement chamber were kept closed during Shudha's month-long confinement and she recalled her terrible thirst and resentment at the rules she had to follow.

When Shudha was ready to give birth to her second child (1921), her family no longer employed Khirodai and instead hired a "real midwife." After two days of difficult labor, this trained midwife urged the family to call a doctor. The doctor summoned was male. After he arrived, the family debated whether or not he could attend Shudha. She was unconscious by the time he entered the birthing room and never saw the man who delivered her son.[66]

Shudha's third confinement was not recorded in her memoirs. In 1935 she entered Elgin Nursing Home instead of returning to her father's house. She did not make this decision for medical reasons but rather to spare her natal family the trouble and expense of arranging for the birth of a child. Moreover, the nursing home had a very good reputation and she looked forward to having a bright and cheerful room all to herself. When she went into labor during the night, the nurse refused to wake up the doctor. By the time he arrived it was too late; her daughter was stillborn. The doctor told her the baby had died because of human error; had he been summoned earlier he could have delivered a healthy baby.[67]

One can see in the pattern of these three births an "enlightened," urban, middle-class family's response to the changing image of the traditional *dhai*. Without empirical evidence that trained midwives and nursing homes could better guarantee a safe birth, Shudha's family sought out these new services, as did others who considered themselves among the "best families."

Women who were married to men who belonged to the Civil Service, for example Saroj Nalini Dutt, Shudha Mazumdar, and Sushama Sen, accompanied their husbands on their postings to the districts. From their memoirs we know they were concerned about medical care for women in the mofussil [rural localities]. They worked, by forming women's groups that could engage in petition politics, to bring Western-trained medical personnel to district towns and villages. Since they were part of the official network they were called upon to sponsor baby weeks and encourage women to learn the rudiments of first aid and childcare. Shudha Mazumdar reported that in Chittagong it was very difficult to entice women in the Mahila Samiti [Women's Association] to exhibit their children in the "baby show." Fearful of attracting the "evil eye," these women saw no reason to participate, so only Shudha, the wives of other officials, and the office peon (whose daughter was six years old) exhibited their children.[68]

The *dhai* became the symbol of superstition and dogged resistance to change. Enamored by science and Western medicine, "new women" wanted lady doctors or nurses. They were not interested in traditional birth attendants because they no longer believed in the rules and rituals surrounding childbirth. Respectability and refinement had replaced purity and pollution in their everyday lives so the old-fashioned *dhai*, with her experience gained from other women and knowledge of *bhuts* [ghosts] and the evil eye, was something of an embarrassment.

Faced with the problem of India's high infant and maternal mortality rate, the answer seemed to be at hand. Poverty and poor living conditions did not become central issues in the women's organizations. The problem was the *dhai*; the solution, providing modern scientific training schemes. The schemes developed were not really designed to train the *dhai*, their purpose was to replace her. The training courses were generally in English and they were presented in a classroom format which would have made it nearly impossible for an adult woman with a midwifery practice to attend the lectures and complete the assignments. Where traditional *dhais* were enticed to begin training schemes, their dropout rate was close to one hundred percent. That any of them completed these courses was truly miraculous, such were the impediments to success.

What the new, trained midwives did was quite different. First, they visited homes and, like doctors, delivered babies and left. Cleaning up the afterbirth and nursing the mother during the days of confinement were not part of their duties. Second, since the majority of them were employed by institutions associated with the government—either in government hospitals run by municipalities, or in new industries in positions mandated by government legislation—their loyalty was to the Raj and its allies, not to the Indian client. When *dhais* resisted both the training schemes and efforts to register and regularize the exercise of their profession they did so in the interest of maintaining traditional standards of care, their own autonomy, and the autonomy of their clients. A different class of Indian women patronized Western medical institutions. The bravest among them fought to enter the new medical system, thereby advancing their autonomy from traditional patriarchy and gender roles.

The introduction of Western medical care for pregnant mothers provides an interesting case study to consider the extension of hegemony in civil society. On the one hand, it leads one to agree with David Arnold that "Ideologically, medicine was a conspicuous part of the self-vindication of colonial rule and of its subordination of Indian society."[69] In this case, middle-class women, at least on the surface, willingly accepted this subordination. But in vindicating hegemony, they were asserting their autonomy. It seems that one must pay at least as much attention to this assertion as to their support of hegemony or miss the complexity unveiled by the historical record.

The mechanics of how hegemony functioned in the construction of the "dangerous *dhai*" is particularly interesting. Hegemony operated, not to change the system of health care, but to describe the *dhai* as a social pathology. But the disease, that is, the *dhai*, resisted all efforts of the Western medical system to render her harmless. In the face of resistance, a symptomology was developed to label this pathology as so vicious and evil as to be beyond treatment. The only remedy was termination. Proponents of Western science, face to face with the *dhai*, had created an ideology, not a system of medicine. Science and medicine had been accepted by and benefited the progressive middle-class, at the same time it undermined the legitimacy of the only caregivers to whom the larger population had access.

Education to Earn[†]
Training Women in the Medical Professions

At the inaugural meeting of the National Association for Supplying Female Medical Aid to the Women of India [also known as the Dufferin Fund], the Viceroy explained that Queen Victoria had issued a special injunction to provide Western medical aid to women trapped in zenanas. Bound to their homes by religion and custom, these women could not see male doctors, he explained, and were at the mercy of "grossly and dangerously ignorant" *dhais*.[1] The solution was to set up women-only hospitals and dispensaries staffed by female doctors and midwives. While it was assumed that a number of professional women would come from England, the Central Committee also planned to train Indian women as doctors and midwives. But in India, female education was a contentious topic. Although many Indians approved of instruction designed to produce ideal wives, most opposed co-education and employment-oriented subjects. Nevertheless, the colonial authorities, in collaboration with the progressive elite, developed programs to educate Indian women in Western medicine, attracted students, and produced a new class of professional women. This essay analyzes the motives of the government and of the Indian men who supported them, the strategies adopted to make these programs work, and their impact on the women who completed them.

[†]Research for this paper was carried out with grants from the State University of New York and the American Institute of Indian Studies. I am indebted to many colleagues for their writings and ideas: Tapan Raychaudhuri, Dagmar Engels, Barbara Ramusack, Antoinette Burton, Rosemary Fitzgerald, Philippa Levine, Supriya Guha, Chandrika Paul, and David Arnold.

EDUCATION FOR WOMEN

"If education has any value for girls," Sarala Ray wrote in 1909, "it must make her more fit for her household work and daily life. Mere theoretical knowledge cannot make her a good wife or a good mother."[2] Ray was not expressing anything new, one of the common criticisms of early schools for girls was that they did not "fit" them for the social and domestic lives they would lead. As a consequence, educators had difficulty attracting girls from influential families who wanted their daughters to marry and devote their time to housework and childcare. After surveying female education in 1848, the Indian Education Commission concluded there was no demand for education as a means of livelihood and that co-education, beyond the primary level, was unacceptable. The Commission recommended grants-in-aid to separate female schools, special prizes and scholarships, and the development of a new curriculum with standards "simpler than those for boys."[3] However, grants-in-aid and scholarships could not dispel prejudice against educational programs that seemed designed to fit women for employment.

That some women worked for wages, either because they belonged to castes that were destined to labor or because misfortune forced them to, was an accepted fact. The problem with formal education, and especially English education, was that it "became entirely synonymous with securing paid employment."[4] The wrong kind of education would lead, it was feared, to independent thinking, competition in the workforce, and finally, the "disintegration of cultural norms."[5]

Despite opposition, the late nineteenth century witnessed a growing acceptance of formal education for women. In the vanguard of this movement were Western-educated men, employed in government service and the new professions, who wanted companionate wives. The product, the "new woman," educated about the home and the world but firmly located in the family, became an essential force in the development of nationalism.[6] For these newly educated women, living under what Judith Walsh has called "new patriarchy," this was personally liberating. Education made it possible for them to participate in shaping their own lives and futures.[7] However, none of these women or their families imagined them using their education to earn a living.

WESTERN MEDICAL EDUCATION IN INDIA

The Indian Medical Service [IMS] was established in 1764 to attend to the medical needs of the British in India. In addition to IMS doctors, the British employed native compounders, dressers, and apothecaries who belonged to the Subordinate Medical Service. By the 1820s, increased demand from the military and civilian populations for Western medicine led to the decision to train "natives" as doctors. Calcutta Medical College [CMC], established in 1835, became the first Indian institution to award medical degrees. According to David Arnold and Mark Harrison, Western medicine became a tool of empire: keeping white masters and colonial subjects healthy, facilitating social control, and creating knowledge that fed a discourse justifying imperialism.[8]

British concern with the medicalized bodies of Indian women dates from the 1860s when venereal disease threatened the fighting capacity of the army. The Contagious Diseases Acts, passed to deal with this problem in British seaports, legalized compulsory fortnightly internal examinations of common prostitutes and the internment in "lock hospitals" of women suffering from gonorrhea or syphilis. The Cantonment Acts applied, with some variation, the same principles to the Empire. In colonies such as India and Hong Kong the sex trade was organized within military cantonments where theoretically all prostitutes were registered and periodically inspected. Infected women were sent to lock hospitals and treated, often with mercury, until the symptoms disappeared. This legislation was designed to protect the health of British soldiers; Indian women were of interest only if they were prostitutes and because they were considered the carriers of debilitating diseases.[9] The records indicate women resisted these examinations as well as the entire system of registration, while officials complained that *dhais* hired to carry out the distasteful inspections were in collusion with the prostitutes.[10]

Western medical care directed at Indian women began in earnest with the missionaries. It was not until the 1860s that single women were grudgingly admitted to the missionary calling but, like the wives and daughters of earlier missionaries, they were to confine their work to women and children.[11] When medical care was added to the missionary repertoire, the Indian custom of purdah created a demand for women doctors. Dr. Clara Swain, an American and the first female medical missionary to India, arrived in 1869. A few years later, Dr. William Elmslie, a British doctor and a pioneer of medical mission work in Kashmir, published a persuasive call for female medical missionaries from England. Before long, missions on both sides of the Atlantic began to champion the ability of women to apply the "double cure:" healing the body while they healed the spirit.[12] These medical missionaries saw the need to train Indian women to assist them and sponsored the first medical training schemes for converts.

But members of the medical establishment believed women medical missionaries created "family discord and strife," and in the process made it difficult for *pardanashin* to obtain the benefits of Western treatment. What was needed, they claimed, were programs to train women and scholarships to support them.[13] Less than two years later the Queen asked the Countess of Dufferin to study the matter and decide what could be done. The Countess of Dufferin's Fund, begun in 1885, became the first program with official support to focus on medical care for Indian women. The Home Department immediately informed municipalities that some of the funds at their disposal could be spent on female hospitals and dispensaries, while other branches of the government lent their support to the educational programs that would train these women.

TRAINING INDIAN WOMEN AS MEDICAL PRACTITIONERS

Midwives and *Dhais*

In 1837 Pandit Madhusudan Gupta recommended that Calcutta Medical College sponsor a program to train midwives and build a lying-in hospital for poor women. Poor women, it was assumed, would come for free treatment and allow medical students to practice what they were learning.[14] Pandit Madhusudan's suggestion materialized as the Midwifery Hospital of CMC. Begun in 1840, this hospital taught male medical students how to use modern instruments such as forceps and ether as an anesthetic. The 1848 report of the Midwifery Hospital proudly announced that their graduates regularly attended confinements in the homes of "respectable Natives" who had abandoned the custom of secluding the new mother and baby in an outhouse or side room.[15] However, these families did not patronize the hospital.

Scattered records inform us that Indian women were being trained in midwifery by the middle of the century but details about these programs are difficult to find. For example, the Government Agent to the Nawab of Carnatic wrote in 1853 about four Muslim women who studied at "Dr. Scott's institution and Lying-in hospital" and received certificates as trained midwives.[16] The Nawab sponsored this initiative but it is not clear if Dr. Scott's hospital regularly held midwifery classes. Margaret Balfour and Ruth Young mention *dhai*-retraining schemes set up by members of the Indian Medical Service that failed because "the young men teachers had probably no practical experience in midwifery."[17] At least one of these, Dr. Aitchison's class for *dhais*, begun in Amritsar in 1866, survived and became the Amritsar Dais' School under the Church of England Zenana Missionary Society.[18] Mitford Hospital in Dacca began training women as midwives in 1870[19] but CMC's plan to begin a course the same year was canceled because they could not find enough pupils. Details about the total number of graduates are difficult to find but one institution, Eden Hospital, trained less than a dozen students a year throughout the 1890s.[20] Clearly these programs could not produce enough midwives to replace traditional birth attendants for Bengal Presidency's adult female population, which exceeded 20 million by this time.

Although a great deal of ink was spilled over the need to retrain the traditional *dhai*,[21] it was extremely difficult for these women to enroll in and complete these courses. To be admitted to "the Sick Nursing Certificate" program, the first step in the process, candidates had to be over 17 years of age, hold a vernacular or Anglo-vernacular Lower Primary certificate, and be of good moral character. The exam for this certificate, taken after a probationary residency of six months, tested their knowledge and practice of elementary sanitation; bed-making; use of simple remedies such as poultices and cold-water dressing, various kinds of baths, application of bandages, slings, and splints; administration of medicines; observation of conspicuous symptoms; and food preparation. Those who passed were enrolled in classes in: anatomy (the female pelvis and the organs and other structures concerned in parturition); signs and symptoms of pregnancy; natural, simple, and complex labor; causes and treatment of excessive hemorrhage; and treatment and management of the newly born infant. In addition to theoretical and practical exams, each candidate was required to assist a doctor at 20 confinements and deliver three infants on her own.[22]

While programs to train midwives were far more successful in Madras, Punjab, Sind, and some native states than in Bengal, [23] it is not clear that any of these programs were successful in making *dhais* into midwives in the way Eden Hospital understood the profession. Because these programs required knowledge of English and regular attendance at a hospital, few practicing *dhais* had the qualifications or the leisure to attempt them. Instead, the courses attracted a new class of women, mostly Indian Christians and Eurasians, with a few Europeans and occasionally a Hindu, Muslim or Brahmo woman from a progressive family.

The demand for trained midwives came from urban and district hospitals and dispensaries, factories, and plantations, not from individual families. Many families preferred the old system, which sometimes found institutional support. Supriya Guha quotes a note from the Civil Surgeon in Dacca, J. Wise to his superiors informing them trained midwives were not allowed to practice by the *mohalladars*. Connected to their duties overseeing neighborhoods, the *mohalladars* supervised *dhais* and taxed them.[24] Dhais were also privileged by traditional relationships with families, the fee differential, and the dubious reputation of midwives. As late as 1902, the Superintendent of the Lady Dufferin Victoria Hospital reported that the *dhais* had "such good practice in Calcutta that so far no bribe has been able to induce them to come [to retraining classes]."[25] Nevertheless, the growing demand from the formal sector, fortified by a rhetoric that held the "dangerous *dhai*" responsible for the high infant and maternal mortality rates, led to new schemes to retrain these women.

Programs to retrain indigenous birth attendants had even more difficulty finding students than the formal midwifery programs. Once they were able to enroll *dhais* in classes, they had to figure out how to re-educate them in Western methods. Reformers argued that to save lives *dhais* only needed to learn the basic principles of hygiene, to recognize excessive bleeding as a danger signal, and when to call for assistance. Enticing them to these classes, even with stipends and bribes, was difficult enough; convincing them of the superiority of Western medicine and the importance of deferring to Western medical practitioners was close to impossible. Moreover, Western-trained doctors were not willing to share "all." The "kits" given to retrained *dhais* contained soap and scissors but not forceps, speculums, or chloroform.[26] Some schemes involved follow-up visits by lady doctors and rewards for successful deliveries, but more often the retrained women had no further contact with their teachers and returned to their old ways.

In 1901 Lady Curzon launched the Victoria Memorial Scholarship Fund to retrain *dhais* to work in zenanas. Dufferin Fund hospitals, clinics, and dispensaries in the districts became the sites for these programs, however, not all 41 hospitals joined the project. In 1902 four institutions had *dhai*-training schemes with a total of 10 pupils and three more had programs but no pupils.[27] The following years were just as disappointing and while there were 15 *dhai* classes in the mofussil in 1909, they had only 65 students. The difficulty, the 1909 report stated, was getting "good pupils."[28] Eight years after this particular program was initiated, they had trained 40 *dhais* for a total of 277. Those in charge of these classes continued to find their pupils ignorant, illiterate, and even hostile to these new ideas.[29]

The lack of attention to retraining *dhais* is especially interesting given the virulence of the rhetoric denouncing them. The attack began early, as early as the 1840s when British doctors decried the torture inflicted on Indian women by *dhais*, and continued into the 1930s and 40s. When half-hearted schemes failed and professional midwifery courses turned out dozens rather than hundreds of graduates, there was little soul searching as to why. Instead, native ignorance and superstition were blamed for the failure of programs that were poorly designed.

One can also doubt the seriousness of colonial authorities and even reformers. A few trained midwives to work as matrons in government hospitals and serve the needs of the urban elite were enough. By the end of the century, many families who had accepted the superiority of Western medicine demonstrated their status by calling the best medical doctors for confinements. These were European men, usually well-known professors at Medical College. Trained midwives sometimes assisted them but it was the male doctor who was credited with the successful delivery. As for the rest of the population, they were characterized as "clinging" to primitive childbearing customs with self-destructive fervor. Chandrika Paul and Supriya Guha have written about the medicalization of childbirth in nineteenth-century Bengal, but I would argue it was only medicalized for the urban elite. Old practices were derided and denounced but no one initiated serious and practical programs to educate and retrain traditional birth attendants in Western medicine.[30]

Meanwhile, Indian reformers were not of one mind when it came to childbirth. Brahmos, who were especially interested in Western medicine, wrote articles urging reform of the birthing process and encouraged the use of both doctors and trained midwives in delivery.[31] Other members of the "progressive class" clung to traditional birthing practices, sometimes claiming they did so in deference to their wives and mothers who presided over the inner quarters. Still others, concerned with status, mixed the two systems and brought male doctors to the *aturghar* [traditional birthing room].[32] Brahmos supported training schemes for midwives, and in fact sent their own wives and daughters to them, but there is no evidence they wanted these programs confused with programs to retrain the traditional *dhai*. Cornelia Sorabji, an outspoken critic of the "progressives," quoted a Brahmo lady's response to the scheme to train *dhais* to treat women in seclusion: "That is pandering to superstition," the woman allegedly said, "let them come out into the open and take what we have or do without and die in seclusion."[33] Sorabji wanted the government to intervene and support hybrid programs to bridge the gap between the common people and Western science.

There is considerable evidence that midwifery-training programs were emancipatory for the women who obtained this credential. Hemangini Das, the wife of Dr. Sundarimohan Das (1857–1950) who received his MB from Calcutta Medical College in 1882, completed the midwifery course in 1880. Sundarimohan, a member of the Sadharan Brahmo Samaj and a close friend of Sibnath Sastri, started a private practice in Sylhet and then Calcutta. In Calcutta, Hemangini accompanied her highly respected husband to confinements until he joined the Medical Department of Calcutta Corporation in 1890. After that, she advertised her services in the newspaper listing her address as "c/o Dr. Sundari Mohan Das, M.B."[34] There are anecdotal accounts that she was respected and successful. Moreover, she was eulogized, in accounts of Sundarimohan's life, as an ideal wife, a "quiet type of woman who was a constant source of inspiration to her husband."[35] Midwives were in demand and an income meant financial independence and some degree of autonomy. There is no data on the re-trained *dhais* but those who refused training or had no opportunity to attend these programs were eventually the losers. Wealthy families replaced traditional *dhais* with trained midwives and lady doctors, while government hospitals and dispensaries employed only trained midwives.

MEDICAL DOCTORS

A few missionary women practiced medicine in India without degrees well before 1870, but Dr. (Miss) Clara Swain, was the first fully qualified medical missionary in India. Fanny Butler, who trained at the London School of Medicine for Women and took her exams in Ireland, came to India in 1880 as the first qualified English woman medical missionary.[36] Fanny belonged to the first class of students to attend the London School of Medicine for Women [LSMW], which opened in 1874. Although the LSMW provided a full course of study, no medical school in the United Kingdom admitted women to the examinations. Three years later, in 1877, the Royal College of Physicians in Ireland opened the examinations to women making it possible for Fanny Butler and her classmates to become qualified doctors.

The perception that foreign medical women were needed in India played an important role in opening medical schools to British women.[37] Just as India gave employment to Britain's "redundant women" as missionaries, it provided jobs for some of the first women doctors who found it difficult to practice at home. The circle was a comfortable one: tales of the zenana provided the *raison d'être* for British women's medical training, trained women pursued lucrative careers in the Empire, and feminism was removed from "home" and given free expression in India where it legitimized British rule. By sponsoring British medical women for women-only hospitals, the Raj posed as both humane and sensitive to the needs of the zenana.

In comparison with England, women in India gained admittance to medical colleges and the medical profession quite easily. Mrs. Scharlieb, an English barrister's wife, came to India in 1866 and, "moved" by the suffering of the women she saw, took a course in midwifery and then applied for admittance to Madras Medical College. In 1875, she and three other women were admitted to the certificate course, a three-year course less rigorous than the MB degree.[38]

Calcutta Medical College, however, proved more resistant to integration. In 1882, Elle D'Abreau and Abala Das applied for admittance to CMC but were turned down because they had passed only the First Arts and not the BA examination. Both were sent to Madras Medical School where they studied for the certificate degree.[39] Chandrika Paul sees this incident as seminal in the movement to admit women to CMC. Editorials deplored both the state of women's education in Bengal and the government's failure to open medical training to women.

In point of fact, it was members of the Council of Medical Colleges and the Calcutta Medical faculty, not the government, who opposed this idea. Women already had a place in medicine, as nurses and midwives, prominent doctors argued. Moreover, women didn't want or need women practitioners, and would not come forward to be trained. Those who enrolled, they argued, would emerge half-educated, steal patients from qualified doctors, and degrade the profession. Even if one recognized a need for female doctors and could find candidates, the government would have to build sex-segregated institutions.[40] Disagreeing, a number of Indian men swore their wives wanted female practitioners and their own daughters intended to study medicine. They joined a strong movement within government to open Calcutta Medical College to women.

In 1883 Kadambini Basu, a BA from Bethune College, applied to Calcutta Medical College and was admitted when the Lieutenant-Governor overruled the Medical Council and consented to the admission of women. Shortly before entering medical school, Kadambini married Dwarkanath Ganguli, her longtime mentor and friend. In 1886 she was awarded the GBMC [Graduate of Bengal Medical College], instead of the more prestigious MB degree, because she had failed one part of her final practical exams.[41] The same year Kadambini entered CMC, Anandibai Joshi sailed from Calcutta to New York, and was taken by her sponsors to enroll in the Women's Medical College in Pennsylvania.[42] Before long, Bombay University agreed to admit non-matriculated women to a three-year certificate course and classes for women began in 1887.[43] In eastern India Miss Bidhumukhi Bose and Miss Virginia Mary Mitter became Calcutta Medical College's first Indian lady graduates in 1890.

Members of the medical profession had not favored admitting women to CMC but government officials overruled them. It seems clear that the medical profession in India was weaker, vis-à-vis government authority, and hence less able to assert its will than was the case in England and other colonies. By 1895, 34 women had graduated from Medical College[44] (see Appendix A). The 21 of these employed by Dufferin Hospitals and the three in private practice could be viewed as part of the project to bring Western medicine to secluded women.

Although the Dufferin hospitals and dispensaries, opened after 1885 with private donations and government support, provided employment for many of these women, some labeled the organization exploitative and discriminatory. In 1891 Kadambini Ganguli, who on three occasions held temporary posts at Calcutta Zenana Hospital and was overlooked for a permanent position, complained the Fund favored foreign women over Indian women. *The Bengalee* grumbled that high positions in the Duff Fund were reserved for European and Eurasian women. The newspaper cited Kadambini's credentials, a BA and a GBMC, as superior to those of any other candidate including the woman hired for the job. *The Bengalee* pointed out that none of the employees of the Bengal Duff Fund had any degree, medical or otherwise.[45] The exclusion of Indian women from the best hospital jobs, Kadambini argued, prevented them from developing their skills:

The Indian medical women will miss all the advantages of such professional duties by their exclusion from the medical charge of important hospitals, or by being placed in an inferior position there, for in the inferior class of hospitals few cases of importance will ever go for treatment, and in the large and important hospitals the major operations and other important duties will always be performed by the senior person in charge.[46]

The opening of more Duff hospitals and dispensaries, mostly in district towns, improved the employment possibilities of women trained in the medical colleges but only if they were willing to accept lower salaries. Medical College graduates expected salaries between Rs. 250 and Rs. 400 a month while most municipalities could pay only Rs. 30 to Rs. 50 per month. By and large it was Indian graduates rather than Europeans or Eurasians who accepted these offers. Clearly, Indian women continued to be disadvantaged in a system that placed men above women, foreign credentials above those earned in India, and discounted knowledge of local languages and customs.

In the twentieth century Indian women began to reap the benefits of their medical education but even then the path was difficult. The Association of Medical Women in India, the body formed in 1907 to work for a Women's Medical Service [WMS] included among its members only a few Indian women and proposed a two-tier system with inferior and superior grades. In urging the government to create the WMS, they focused attention on the *pardanashin*, insisting it was the duty of the Raj to provide medical services to the daughters of the Empire. While these arguments should have benefited Indian women doctors, they were in fact marginalized since the plan rewarded medical credentials and knowledge of English above local knowledge. The WMS, set up in 1914, presented new opportunities for women to gain status, prestige, and financial independence but only if they had the right qualifications. While opening medical colleges to women can be read as a decision to place gender above race in the delivery of medical relief, it was a program that raced gender by placing British women above Indian women. It was not until 1947 that an Indian woman, Dr. Hilda Lazarus (an Indian Christian), held the position of Chief Medical Officer of the WMS.

Opening training in Western medicine to Indian women was a consequence of demands by Indian progressives, receptive officials, and a climate of opinion that thought it the Raj's duty to "bid the sickness cease." Medical men, both Indian and British, at first opposed bringing women into medical colleges but the argument that trained women were needed to treat *pardanashin* won the day.

While this training brought women doctors professional prestige and financial rewards, the downside was the negative public perception of women who mixed with men in medical school and traveled alone. Some women encountered sexual harassment, threats of rape, and even abduction. Much has been made of the fact that the newspaper *Bangabasi* caricatured a man led "by the nose" by his prostitute-wife. When the newspaper confirmed the man was Dwarkanath Ganguli, this was considered the same as calling Kadambini a whore.[47] Other women, for example, Virginia Mary Mitter, gave up their practices after marriage because their husbands opposed their employment. Still others, like Dr. Jamini Sen, remained single and had long careers. Jamini, who graduated in 1896 at age 25 with both the LMS and MB, was the only Bengali girl in her Medical College class. She won distinction in her fourth year, receiving a first in Materia Medica, bested only by her classmate

*Dr. Jamini Sen, LMS
and MB from Calcutta
Medical College 1894.
c. 1903 (Bijoy Chandra
Majumdar Collection.
Courtesy Sevati Mitra.)*

Rachael Cohen who received the Gold Metal in Botany and a
first in Anatomy.[48] After graduation, Jamini went to Nepal where
she worked in Bir Hospital and attended the royal family. Parul
Bose, who knew Jamini as a friend of her parents, said she used to
cover her head to look more "dignified." Asked why Jamini remained
single, Parul replied: "sometimes girls just did not want to marry."[49]
Overall, the picture seems to be more positive than negative but
the biographies of these women have not yet been written.

HOSPITAL ASSISTANTS

The third program to train women as medical professionals
produced Hospital Assistants. The Vernacular Licentiate in Medicine
and Surgery [VLMS] prepared women with very little formal

education to "assist" doctors. Calcutta was not the earliest site for these programs although it became one of the largest.[50]

Proposals to admit women to Campbell Medical School date from the 1870s when Neel Kamal Mitra, who held this degree, petitioned to have his granddaughter Biraj Mohini enrolled. Mitra insisted Biraj Mohini be given a curtained-off seat, apart from the male students, and taught dissection in a separate room with her husband (a student at CMC) or himself present.[51] The reply to his request has not been preserved but we know Biraj Mohini did not attend any classes. Most medical professionals responded negatively to these requests arguing there were very few candidates for this training. Repeating sentiments voiced when women sought admittance to CMC, they argued that native women, "steeped in ignorance and tradition," did not want Western medical care. [52] However, their greatest fear was that these half-trained women would "discredit the Western system of medicine."[53] Nevertheless, members of the Sadharan Brahmo Samaj convinced Campbell Medical School's Superintendent that there was demand for women hospital assistants and women who wanted to be trained. The Director of Public Instruction supported the idea and developed a plan that included everything from admittance standards to scholarships and classroom decorum.[54]

Campbell Medical School, the major institution to train men as Hospital Assistants for the Subordinate Medical Service, admitted its first batch of women students in 1888, five years later than Calcutta Medical College but with 15 women instead of one. The women who attended CMC were mostly Christians, Eurasians, and Europeans, with an occasional Brahmo, while Campbell's classes included Hindus and Muslims alongside their Brahmo, Christian, and Eurasian classmates. The numbers seeking admission remained high, prompting *The Indian Messenger* to comment that a "craving for lucrative and useful occupations is daily rising among the indigent class of middle-class Hindu women."[55] By 1894 Campbell had about 300 pupils, with over two-thirds of them enrolled in the VLMS, the others in the compounder class. Of those in the VLMS program, only seven percent were women, the rest were men destined for careers in government-related industries.

Entering Campbell with very little formal education, the women had a failure rate considerably higher than the men. By 1893 about half of the men entering the program had studied up to university entrance and 98 percent of them knew English while only two percent of the women had passed the upper primary examination.[56] Nevertheless, Campbell's Superintendent reported that "the girls" were doing well and all involved were pleased the experience "proved that it is possible to educate male and female students in the same classes without friction or any loss of discipline."[57] As the government raised standards, the program became less diverse and Christian and Eurasian women, with more formal schooling, edged out the Hindu and Muslim girls who attended in the earlier years.

There can be no doubt these graduates played an important role in bringing Western medicine to the districts of Bengal. Bound to service by their scholarships, many of them returned to their home districts to practice for the rest of their lives. Others tried to compete with CMC graduates in Calcutta for private patients, and when they failed accepted mofussil jobs as their second choice. For whatever reason, they became the backbone of these small hospitals and dispensaries, staffing almost 90 percent of those set up by the Dufferin Fund as well as a number of government institutions.

We can track the careers of those who accepted jobs in Dufferin or government hospitals through the Dufferin reports and the annual and triennial *Returns of the Charitable Dispensaries under the Government of Bengal and the Calcutta Medical Institutions*. The sources are more revealing than those we have on trained midwives, who worked with a range of institutions, or medical doctors, many of whom left Bengal to work in native states or went into private practice. In addition to information about their careers, these records tell us about their patients: who was treated and where, and the kind of medicine they delivered.

My concern here is not these details but rather the interplay of the Raj and Indian reformers in opening this particular educational program to women and its emancipatory nature for the women themselves. As was the case in admitting women to

CMC, Indian men supported officials against the objections of medical professionals. While Brahmos were keen about both Western medicine and programs to train widows for useful careers, Campbell's program appealed to a wider range of communities than at first expected. The flexible (read this as minimal) requirements, scholarships, and careful provision for housing, travel, and seating arrangements helped to overcome misgivings about impropriety.

Although these women held "inferior" degrees, they were often put in charge of the hospitals that employed them. There they were supervised by Civil Surgeons with the degree of supervision depending on the individual and the location of the hospital. Practicing in a women's hospital was a respectable career and provided a degree of protection from sexual harassment, but only a degree since they were at the mercy of their male supervisors, and the husbands and guardians of their clients. Salaries were relatively low (though higher than those of men with the same credentials) but could be supplemented by private practice, allowed by most district hospitals and dispensaries.

Whether or not this training was emancipatory is more difficult to answer. Haimabati Sen, a childless and destitute widow who had no one to care for her, was not unlike many of her classmates. Looking at the ages of the women who entered Campbell, one can assume that most of them were widows and that many were caring for children. Only a few Christians girls, listed as "Miss," were under 17 years of age, while many of the Hindu and Brahmo women were in their late 20s and early 30s. These were the women *The Indian Messenger* referred to as from the "indigent class of middle-class Hindu women" who they hoped could be trained to do useful work. Even though she remarried, Haimabati's husband did not support her and it was first her scholarship, and then her salary, that provided for the family. Like her, her colleagues gained financial security from their jobs. We do not know the details of their lives but in Haimabati's case, professional employment did not solve all her problems. Despite her position, she suffered from sexual harassment, domestic abuse, and the strains of double work.

CONCLUSIONS

Those who favored formal education wanted to create "new women"—ideal helpmates, knowledgeable about the home and the world, yet dedicating their lives to building the new family for the new nation. Most of the women who are remembered by historians did not use their education to earn a living but rather remained in their homes and devoted their spare time to writing, women's organizations, social uplift, and the arts. In contrast, medical education was designed to prepare women to work outside the home for wages. Whether it was meant for midwives, doctors, or hospital assistants, it forced the recipients to play in-between roles, dependent on the Raj for their education and in many cases their jobs, and dependent on their families for status and support in their new roles.

While Indian men had to agree initially to allow their female relatives to attend these training programs, graduates practiced medicine away from family control and could become financially independent. Professionally they had considerable autonomy but they were always answerable to English and Indian men who held positions in the Indian Medical Service. However, there is little to suggest that professional autonomy went hand-in-hand with either personal freedom or familial independence. Furthermore, their professional positions prevented them from openly criticizing the government just as these positions mandated personal respectability.

These efforts to provide education for employment stand as an anomaly among other nineteenth-century programs to educate Bengali women. Issues such as a curriculum suitable for females, separate schools, and women instructors were not discussed at this time.[58] However, neither were issues associated with employment such as salaries and terms of service. Instead, medical education for women was validated in terms of service to humanity. In the resolution to admit Kadambini to Calcutta Medical College, the Lieutenant-Governor stated that it was "natural and reasonable" for Indian women to want to "enter a profession which would find, in India … a wide sphere of action and of beneficent service." Instead of discussing the work of the women doctors, he focused on the clients:"women in every position of life who would prefer death to treatment by a male physician."[59]

By reiterating essentialist views about women's nature, government officials and reformers rationalized a curriculum for women doctors that would be the same for both sexes and taught in the same classroom. In contrast, the midwifery programs were designed for women only. Because these new practitioners would treat only women, they did not appear to be taking "men's jobs" or competing with men. At the same time, the sites where they practiced, women-only hospitals and private homes, theoretically offered them the protection women needed and desired. The women, many of whom pursued education primarily because they needed to earn a living, were captives of this discourse. Earning an income must have given them some bargaining power within their families but we do not know how much. Because their work roles were the creation of imagined desire (of purdah women for medical care), they never practiced medicine outside of male control.

The British had long regarded the zenana as a dangerous place: to its inhabitants because it was a sanctuary of dirt and disease, and to the Raj, because it fostered intrigue and conspiracy. Deciding to extend medical care to Indian women, British officials were convinced they could create new purdah institutions and thereby become the protectors of secluded women. Maneesha Lal has written that the Dufferin Fund acted "to constrain later efforts that might have proven more attuned to the needs of the population of Indian women."[60] British officials supervised these new medical women and the care they provided, but it is equally true that traditional and reinscribed attitudes about women's sphere limited what these women could do. At the same time, evidence indicates the plan—to use Western medicine to bring zenana women under government control—did not work. To bring more women into contact with Western medicine, officials relented and allowed the new medical professionals to treat patients in their own homes, spaces beyond the authority of the Raj but not beyond the authority of Indian patriarchs. Nevertheless, efforts to train Indian women in medicine benefited the hundreds of thousands of women and children who called on their services, and to a certain extent, Indian women seeking professional opportunities.

APPENDIX A

1895: The Careers of Female Doctors from Medical College[61]

Name	Graduated	Employment
1. Miss Ada Niebel	1889	Dufferin Fund—Bhopal
2. Miss L.E. Sykes	1890	England
3. Miss F. Dissent	1890	Nizam's Territory
4. Miss G.F. Pereira	1890	Dufferin Fund—Chittagong
5. Miss L.B. Smith	1890	Private Practice—Calcutta
6. Miss J. Pery	1890	Dufferin Fund—Gaya
7. Miss L. Kirkpatrick	1890	Dufferin Fund—Gaya
8. Miss A. D'Souza	1890	Dufferin Fund—Amritsar
9. Miss Ida M. Dissent	1890	unemployed
10. Miss W. Jahans	1890	Dufferin Fund—Cawnpore
11. Miss Ida Brown	1890	Dufferin Fund—Berhampur
12. Miss J.B. Muller	1891	Dufferin Fund—Karnal
13. Miss H. Forbes	1891	Dufferin Fund—Rangoon
14. Miss M. Scott	1891	Dufferin Fund—Berhampur
15. Miss C. Brooking	1891	unemployed
16. Mrs. J.C. Smythe	1891	England
17. Miss L.M. Carroll	1893	Dufferin Fund—Balarampur
18. E.L. Bridge	1893	Australia
19. Miss S.E. Bridge	1893	Dufferin Fund—Lucknow
20. Miss M.S. Martin	1893	Dufferin Fund—Calcutta
21. Miss T. T. Watts	1893	unemployed
22. Miss K. O'Byrne	1893	Dufferin Fund—Fyzabad
23. Miss L. Blong	1893	Dufferin Fund—Bara Banki
24. Miss D.E. Pratt	1893	Dufferin Fund—Agra
25. Miss J. George	1893	Dufferin Fund—Aligarh
26. Miss S. Anthonie	1893	Dufferin Fund—Quetta
27. Miss A. Lisle	1893	Dufferin Fund—Mooltan
28. Miss G. Woods	1893	Dufferin Fund—Meerut
29. Mrs. N. Neal	1894	unemployed
30. Miss E. George	1894	unemployed
31. Miss A. Imrie	1895	unemployed
32. Miss Mitter	1890	private practice—Calcutta
33. Miss B.M. Bose	1890	private practice—Calcutta
34. Miss B.B. Bose	1890	private practice—Calcutta

Medicine for Women
"Lady Doctors" in the Districts of Bengal

Srimati Hemangini Debi,[1] the lady doctor[2] in charge of the women's hospital, "continued to do her work to the satisfaction of all concerned," wrote the secretary of the Bankura Branch of the Dufferin Fund in 1894. He went on, "She is intelligent and painstaking and appears to prove a great acquisition to the medical staff of this district, affording medical relief to those to whom male doctors could not have much access."[3] Before the end of the century, women's hospitals employing Western-trained women doctors were found in every district of Bengal. These doctors were not graduates of Calcutta Medical College holding the degree of Bachelor of Medicine or the less rigorous Certificate, they were Hospital Assistants trained at Campbell Medical School in Calcutta or Agra Medical School.

By 1903 Bengal Presidency had 43 purdah hospitals and dispensaries funded by the National Association for Supplying Female Medical Aid to the Women of India (also known as the Dufferin Fund), municipal governments, and various charities.[4] Western medical care for Indian women had begun with missionaries who claimed the majority of Indian women were "debarred," by custom, from seeing male doctors or visiting government hospitals and dispensaries. Colonial officials appropriated this discourse when they decided to support the Dufferin Fund's program. By respecting "the different customs and prejudices of our high-caste Hindu and Muhammadan patients,"[5] the Raj could help suffering women while demonstrating concern for its Indian subjects. These facilities were not intended for all women, but specifically for women who observed purdah and belonged to "good" families. If a patient were well off, her family could call a lady doctor for a home visit; if she were seriously ill or the family could not afford the lady doctor's fees, she could be admitted to a women-only hospital. But poor and tribal women, especially those laboring in factories and plantations, were not welcome. It was assumed they were less modest and lacked the delicate sensibilities of their upper-class and upper-caste sisters and could be treated by male doctors.

The "lady doctors" who took up positions at Bankura, the Female Ward of the Dumraon Raj Hospital, the Kandi Girish Chunder Hospital in Murshidabad, the Mymensingh Bidyamoyee Female Hospital, and other district purdah hospitals have not been included in histories of colonial medicine. Historians have written about important members of the Indian Medical Service and medical missionaries, and, more recently, retrieved the careers of prominent British, American, and Indian women doctors, but ignored these lady doctors.[6] I believe their role in bringing Western medicine to women in the mofussil has been overlooked because historians assumed "hospital assistants" occupied only lowly positions. The focus of this essay is these women, as students at Campbell Medical School in Calcutta in the late nineteenth century, and as lady doctors in the districts of Bengal.

LADY DOCTORS

Campbell Admits Women

Campbell Medical School (first called Sealdah Medical School) opened in 1872 to accommodate a Bengali vernacular class that had grown too large for Medical College. Unlike the English-language program at Calcutta Medical College, where the instructors had been educated in Great Britain, Campbell teachers were Indians trained in India. Classes were taught in the vernacular with textbooks written in Bengali or, when these were not available, translations of English texts.[7] Graduates received the Vernacular

Licentiate in Medicine and Surgery and were commonly known as "Hospital Assistants."[8]

Proposals to include women began in the 1870s and by the end of the decade they were allowed to attend lectures but the official records regarding this decision have been destroyed.[9] Serious efforts to set up a vernacular program for women began only after the Dufferin Fund was established and Indian women entered Medical College.

The Dufferin Fund, begun in 1885, became the first program with official support to focus on medical care for Indian women. The Fund's mission was to provide scholarships, train doctors, nurses, and midwives, and sponsor hospitals and dispensaries for women. At the same time, district boards collected funds to build women's hospitals that would be run in collaborate with the Duff Fund and staffed by Duff doctors. The first recruits were British women doctors and graduates of Calcutta Medical College but neither wanted to work where they were most needed—in the districts, or for the low wages proposed. These women stayed in the cities where they worked in large urban hospitals or engaged in private practice, or they accepted positions in native states. In either case, they could easily command salaries ten times those offered by district boards. If the Duff Fund were to fulfill its mission, it needed to find another supply of women doctors.

When Bengali gentlemen first proposed educating women as hospital assistants, British officials doubted there would be suitable applicants. They named "culture" the culprit, arguing that religious beliefs, caste rules, superstitions about female education, and norms of female seclusion would prevent Indian women from attending medical schools.

What the British missed were changes in Bengali society that challenged this static assessment of women's roles. The Sadharan Brahmo Samaj, formed after a split with what they considered their more socially conservative colleagues, loudly proclaimed its vision of public roles for women and encouraged women to form clubs and associations. By the mid-1870s progressive families were sending their daughters to school. Calcutta University allowed women to take the entrance exam in 1878 and the same year,

Bethune College opened to accommodate the students who had passed this exam and wanted to continue their studies. Women writers such as Swarnakumari Debi were publishing novels and writing for *Bharati*, a journal for women.[10] When the Indian National Congress met in Bombay in 1889 there were ten women in attendance including Swarnakumari Debi and Kadambini Ganguli. The next year these two women attended the Congress session in Calcutta as delegates.[11] This phenomenon was not without powerful critics but efforts to modernize women's roles were clearly underway.

It was members of the Sadharan Brahmo Samaj who convinced Coull Mackenzie, Campbell's Superintendent, that opening the school's doors to women would work.[12] The Director of Public Instruction, Sir A.W. Croft, supported the idea and developed a plan that included everything from admittance standards to scholarships and classroom decorum. Because women had little access to formal education, he proposed flexible admission standards. Pass marks in at least two subjects of a newly designed entrance exam, the middle scholarship exam, or the upper primary exam was acceptable for admittance. The special entrance exam, designed for women without formal schooling, required candidates to read and explain a Bengali book of the same level of difficulty as Rajkristo Mukherji's *History of Bengal*; take dictation in Bengali from an easy book; and do arithmetic and fractions to the rule of three. Croft recommended a minimum age for admittance of 16 but no upper age limit in contrast to the rules for men which set an upper limit of age 23. To make this program even more attractive, he endorsed ten scholarships of Rs. 7 per month (males received only Rs. 5 per month), free tuition for others who passed the exam, and special prizes of Rs. 18 for the best student in each subject.[13] Women were to complete the same course as men, but they sat in the front seats of lecture halls, attended dissection class in a screened-off room, and were excused from night duty in the hospital. If they came from the mofussil, there was space for them in Swarnamoyee hostel,[14] while Calcutta women could ride to Campbell in a horse-drawn omnibus. Croft assured the Lieutenant-Governor the costs of this program could be met by a grant from the Education Department.[15]

By the time the arrangements had been made to admit females, Mr. Mackenzie had the names of 15 "serious applicants," from "the most respectable Brahmo families of Bengal." He predicted these women would prove as useful to the province as Campbell's male graduates, men who performed "medical duties on terms that no medical graduate would accept" in tea gardens, factories, railways, and government service.[16]

Not everyone in the medical profession agreed. Surgeon-Major Crombie, Superintendent of Dacca Medical School, scoffed at the idea. Native women were "steeped in ignorance and tradition," he wrote, and did not want Western medical care. Moreover, there would be no candidates for this training. He carefully listed the "facts": respectable Muslim women could not mix freely; Hindu girls married young and immediately had children; and native Christian and Brahmo women could not live among and treat Hindus or Muslims.[17]

Surgeon-Major C.J.W. Meadows, the officiating Civil Surgeon at Patna, worried about lowering standards by licensing a new class of women doctors. The women who passed the entrance exam would not be able to understand medical concepts and, as practitioners, they would "discredit the Western system of medicine."[18]

Dr. R. L. Dutt, Officiating Civil Surgeon of Rungpore and one of the two Bengalis to comment on Croft's plan, agreed with his colleagues. Citing twenty years experience practicing medicine in Bengal, Dr. Dutt claimed no one in the districts wanted women doctors nor would decent women study medicine. But these were minor issues compared with his fear the program would "bring European medicine into disrepute."[19] Clearly the most dangerous aspect of this scheme was its potential to discredit Western medicine and those trained in it.

Letters from district boards and applications from Brahmo women constituted evidence the plan would work. In the end, officials triumphed over medical practitioners. On December 25, 1887, the *Indian Messenger* reported: "Campbell Medical School authorities were given permission to admit girls from the beginning of next season."

In 1888, fifteen Hindu, Brahmo, native Christian, and Eurasian women enrolled in Campbell Medical School and began their study of Western medicine with lectures and textbooks in the Bengali language. Ten received scholarships, five fee waivers.[20] Many had thought the program would appeal only to Brahmo and native Christian women but this was not the case. In the first two years there were more Hindu women, mostly Brahmins and Kayasthas, than Brahmos or native Christians. In 1891 the first Muslim student was admitted, the second came in 1893.

Beginning in 1890, all candidates were required to pass a special elementary exam in English,[21] and the composition of the entering class began to change. Although the program continued to attract Bengali women from all communities through the 1890s, the number of Hindus, Brahmos, and Muslims declined after 1896 when this became a four-year program. By this time at least half of the new students were Bengali Christians. The number of native Christian, European, and Eurasian women continued to increase as the program became more selective and a greater understanding of English was required. By 1905 Curzon's new educational policy,

Female students at Campbell Medical School, 1889. (National Association for Supplying Female Medical Aid to the Women of India)

designed to reassert colonial control over education, had effected a change in the composition of the Campbell's female body.

There can be little doubt about the impact of this program on the province. Between 1891, the year the first student graduated and 1905, when the program required more formal schooling, Campbell produced over 50 Bengali women hospital assistants, the majority of whom accepted positions in the mofussil. According to the 1904 report of the Bengal branch of the Dufferin Fund, 38 of the Fund's 43 female hospitals and dispensaries were under women who had earned the VLMS degree and most were graduates of Campbell Medical School.[22]

The Students

Although we know very little about the lives of these lady doctors, one Campbell graduate, Haimabati Sen, left a detailed and frank account of her education and work as a doctor.[23] Born Haimabati Ghosh in Khulna district of eastern Bengal, *c.* 1866, she was the eldest daughter of a wealthy zamindar [a landed proprietor]. Married at age 10 and widowed within a year, Haimabati spent the next eight years struggling to survive. Her parents and mother-in-law died, her brother stole what was rightfully hers, and her brothers-in-law asked her to leave their home. During these troubled years she continued to study whenever she could and learned enough to become a teacher at a small school for girls in Benares. After hearing about Brahmo Samaj efforts to educate widows, Haimabati made her way to Calcutta.

Haimabati hoped to be admitted to one of the Samaj-sponsored homes where widows lived and received an education. In Calcutta she met two illustrious Sadharan Brahmo Samaj leaders, Sibnath Sastri and Durgamohun Das, but they were leaving for England and unable to help her. Unfortunately, there were more candidates than space at the few widows' homes and Haimabati was sent to live with a family in eastern Bengal. Nearly two years passed before she could return to Calcutta and resume her studies and by this time she had agreed to marry a second time.

In Calcutta, other young widows told Haimabati about Campbell's program to train women hospital assistants. Since her second husband, Kunjabehari Sen, an idealistic and irresponsible missionary, expected her to fend for herself, a medical career seemed ideal. The Rs. 7 scholarship would support their household while she studied; after graduation, she would be able to earn. She asked for and received her husband's permission to prepare for the entrance exam, passed the test, and in 1891 enrolled in Campbell Medical School with 12 other women.[24]

Haimabati's batch resembled previous classes in terms of community and age at time of admittance, but differed by including Campbell's first Muslim student: Mussamut Idennessa from Mymensingh. This class, according to the report, included nine Hindus, nine Christians, seven Brahmos, and one Muslim. In terms of age, Idennessa and Benoy Kumari Chuckerbutty were only 16 years old; the two oldest students were 29. Haimabati Sen was 26, somewhat older than the average age of 21 years. It is not clear how many of these women were admitted on the basis of the special exam, but government reports discuss the desirability of raising standards and the difficulty of doing so. Inadequate academic preparation took its toll: of the 13 women who sat for the first year class exams with Haimabati, six passed and seven failed.[25] Her graduating class totaled four.

The program at Campbell was divided into two parts with exams conducted at Calcutta Medical College at the end of the second and third year. During the first two years students concentrated on anatomy and physiology, and materia medica; in the last year they studied surgery, medicine, therapeutics, midwifery, and medical jurisprudence. Haimabati remembered their difficulties with unintelligible and absentee professors. Because books were difficult to obtain, she and two friends purchased them second-hand from men students and studied together.

Dissection class was especially stressful. The first dissection classes at Medical College used animal parts, wooden models, and tin representations in recognition of Hindu sensibilities. By this time, though, human cadavers were used,[26] so men and women, although they heard lectures in the same classroom, were taught dissection in different rooms. This class must have been distasteful for both sexes, but notions of modesty made it additionally difficult for female students. Haimabati wrote about her "extreme anxiety" the day before dissection and how the sight of a mangled male body made her want to vomit. When she and her student-partner broke into tears, a kindly professor put the knife in her hand, guided her in her first movements, and told her to think of the corpse as an "animal." It was his kindness that helped her through the experience.

This example, not the only one in Haimabati's memoir about solicitous Bengali instructors, contrasts with accounts of British lecturers. In fact, it was rumored that the shift to Sealdah occurred because a Bengali student was falsely accused of stealing medicine. There are many other accounts of racism, discrimination, and genuine meanness. Haimabati recalled an examination at Medical College where the English doctor took obvious delight in humiliating native students.

The lives of Campbell women students were very difficult. Those who lived outside Calcutta had to find a place to live. Some stayed at Swarnamoyee hostel where the majority of the residents were European, Eurasian, and native Christian; others lived in private houses: sharing space with other medical students or boarding with families. Those who stayed at the hostel ate their meals there, the others had to add food preparation to their tasks. Widowed mothers and wives with young children faced the additional problem of childcare. One of Haimabati's classmates, Kadambini Banerji, was a young widow with four children. They lived on charity and her scholarship, but after two years of trying to pass the exams she gave up. Their examiners assumed the women failed because they were poorly prepared and lacked "staying power."[27] They were oblivious to the day-to-day hardships of most of the students.

Lady Doctors

The vernacular degree equipped men and women to be hospital assistants, yet often a Campbell graduate became the "lady doctor in-charge" of a women's hospital. Civil surgeons oversaw their work, performed major operations, and submitted yearly reports on expenditures, patients treated, and quality of their work. Most of the reports were favorable, citing increases in the numbers of patients and the popularity of the doctors. However, the civil surgeons criticized these women for employing men in their establishments and not observing strict purdah. They knew women from well-off families did not want to be treated in hospital wards, but continued to suggest segregated cottages and other measures to attract this class. Because of their superior credentials, the Civil Surgeons performed the major operations in the hospitals in clear violation of purdah rules. They insisted these women doctors were not qualified to perform complex procedures, although they knew women doctors performed major surgery in private homes. Unfortunately the records are silent about their inconsistent and even contradictory statements.

Campbell graduates had an easy time finding positions in the new women's hospitals and dispensaries being built in the districts of Bengal. Those who graduated a year before Haimabati found lucrative positions. For example, Bonotosini Chunder went to Sylhet with a salary of Rs 40 per month, free quarters, and servants; Sushila Debi accepted an appointment at the Lady Dufferin Hospital at Bhagalpur with Rs 60 per month, a horse allowance of Rs 15 per month, and free quarters; and Lukhimoni Debi went to the Monghyr Charitable Dispensary for Rs 50 per month and benefits. Those who had accepted scholarships from district boards, for example, Nistarini Chuckerbutty and Mussamut Idennessa, agreed to return to their districts.[28]

Many of these women had careers as long or longer than men belonging to the Indian Medical Service. In 1903, seven women who had received the VLMS between 1891 and 1894 were still practicing in the districts of Bengal: Haimabati Sen in Hooghly, Mussamut Idennessa in Mymensingh, Hemangini Debi at the Lady Dufferin Hospital in Bankura, Menaka Devi at the Girish Chandra Hospital in Murshidabad; Nistarini Chuckerbutty in the Dumraon Raj Hospital, Shahabad; and Priya Bala Guha in the Zuharunissa Female Hospital, Bogra.[29] Haimabati's career spanned four decades from her appointment to Hooghly Dufferin Hospital, 1894 to 1910, and her subsequent private practice in Chinsurah, from 1910 until her death in 1933. Mussamut Idennessa was the "Native Lady Doctor" of Bidyamoyi Female Hospital in Mymensingh for at least 20 years. There can be no doubt that these women became important and valued members of the communities where they practiced.[30]

Most district hospitals and dispensaries encouraged women doctors to have private patients. Their salaries were generally higher than those paid to their male classmates, but only about one-tenth of the salary earned by foreign-trained doctors or Medical College graduates. These highly qualified women commanded beginning salaries of at least Rs 300 per month plus benefits. Private practice helped even the score for those with inferior credentials since hospital assistants often received Rs. 300–Rs. 400 a month from patients visited in their homes.

Campbell's women graduates found positions easily, were well paid, and often had long and productive careers, but their professional lives were not easy. While those who opposed opening Campbell to women, claiming there would be no demand for this education or for lady doctors, were proved wrong, other difficulties appeared. Sexual harassment, from doctors and other men, was a fact of life. Haimabati Sen wrote about the advances of the doctor in charge of the adjacent male hospital and Promilla Roy, the doctor in charge of the female ward of the Malda English Bazaar Hospital, left her post after she was "maltreated by a zamindar."[31] In other cases, public attitudes hampered their work. In Pabna, for example, the *palki* bearers called the lady doctor a *dhai* and refused to take her to see patients. Without transportation, she was unable to visit women in their homes.[32] But what most affected their careers was their lack of formal education. Even before Campbell admitted these women, members of the medical profession worried about their ability to understand medicine. Although they received high marks for their performance and, according to the records, cured as many patients as male doctors, they were criticized for not treating more patients in their hospitals. It was assumed patients stayed away from women's hospitals because the lady doctors were only hospital assistants. By 1903 the civil surgeons were pushing for higher admittance standards, internships at established hospitals, and women inspectresses. Most of these agreed, wrote Mr. Carstairs in a report on Dufferin hospitals, that "defective education" explained the "inefficiency" of the lady doctors.[33]

THE PATIENTS

Where were women treated?

The British understood the purdah system as a rigid and imputable set of rules that prohibited interaction between unrelated men and women. When missionaries realized male converts could not deliver their families, they sent missionary women into the zenanas. They first taught literary and religious education, then practiced simple medicine. Before long, missionaries complained that it was difficult to monitor treatment and impossible to tell patients about Christ in their dirty and disorganized homes. As Rosemary Fitzgerald has pointed out, they preferred hospitals and dispensaries where they could accomplish more medically and spiritually.[34]

British officials also preferred hospitals and dispensaries as these institutions demonstrated the benevolence of their rule. Women, oppressed by custom and kept ignorant by purdah, could be brought into contact with the Raj only, so it was reasoned, through institutions that respected the need for sex-segregation. But rigid sex-segregation included separating women who observed purdah from those who did not or could not because they had to work outside the home. Reports about the various institutions repeated the importance of reserving hospital space for *pardanashin* and excluding men from the premises.

The Hooghly Dufferin Women's hospital opened in 1894 and after losing its first lady doctor, hired Haimabati Sen. Located in the old Chinsurah barracks, this hospital shared the building with the relocated Imambara Hospital which previously treated both men and women. When the hospital opened it had four patients, transferred from the old hospital, all of whom were indigent and chronically ill. In her early years, Dr. Sen treated about 230 patients per year in the hospital, about fifteen times that number in the outdoor clinic, and approximately 150 patients in their homes. It is especially interesting that treating patients at home, a practice that blatantly violated the ideology of the hospital, was encouraged. D.B. Allen, the district magistrate for Hooghly, reported in 1896,

Considering the great difficulty in getting middle-class or high-caste women into the hospital for treatment, the method adopted by the Lady-Doctor of gratuitously attending poor women at home has been eminently successful, and will likely make this institution popular.[35]

Ten years later Dr. Sen was treating almost 400 patients in her hospital, and close to 6,000 in the outdoor clinic. But her home visits had also grown and now numbered over 270.[36] In other areas, women continued to shun the hospital. Reports from Dacca and Mymensingh confirm that lady doctors treated more than ten times as many women in their homes as in the hospital.[37]

In district after district civil surgeons reported that most "Hindu ladies of good social position" asked the doctors to come to their homes.[38] Home care had distinct advantages. It maintained and in some cases enhanced family status, was undoubtedly safer, and insured patriarchal control. Even the Lady Dufferin Victoria Hospital in Calcutta had difficulty attracting patients. Their reports are full of apologies and excuses for the low attendance. Among other things, they blamed the location of the hospital, the unsavory reputation of the nurses, and hospital rules that required patients to stay for three days. While the numbers seeking medical care increased every year, "respectable" women did not attend outdoor clinics or enter hospitals. A summary of women treated by Duff hospitals from 1894 to 1907 counted approximately 492,000 women treated in hospitals and 368,000 treated at home.[39]

The picture is clear: large numbers of women and children attended out-patient clinics, a fraction of this number were treated in hospitals, and a slightly smaller number were treated in their homes. Officials tolerated home care as the first step in reaching secluded women, but it was obvious medicine was not effective in opening the zenana. This meant that Western medicine was practiced in spaces where colonial authority did not reach.

Who received treatment?

The question of who was treated is extremely important in assessing the extent to which the Campbell experiment served women's needs. This question is also relevant for determining the success of the Raj's project to control women through medical care.

Official government reports at the turn of the century list the total number of patients treated in all government, government-supported, and private hospitals and dispensaries in Bengal as only slightly over three million.[40] Women patients numbered half a million, children only slightly more than that figure, and the remainder were men. Dufferin Fund patients (women and children) numbered about 185,000 or less than 20 percent of the total treated.[41]

Contrary to the propaganda of the Dufferin Fund and others promoting zenana hospitals, government and other charitable institutions had always treated women. And indigenous male practitioners treated many women. The few accounts we have of women patients in government hospitals, suggest they did not enter these hospitals of their own accord but were admitted by their male guardians or the authorities.

Hooghly Dufferin Hospital received funding from the municipality and was responsible for treating any woman deposited there by the police. During plagues they were inundated with patients, but even in normal times they had to admit the indigent sick and dying. In 1897, the deputy magistrate reported the women's hospital was full of "half-starved 'Beharis' and semi-Hinduized aborigines who came to town looking for employment." He complained that even though this influx of patients would boost attendance records, they were not the right kind of patients for two reasons. First, they were definitely not *pardanashin* and second, they would increase the hospital's mortality rates.[42] This is not the only account that deplored the class of in-patients this and other hospitals attracted. Civil Surgeons protested regularly that many women patients did not observe the rules of purdah and could just as well have been treated in a hospital that also admitted men.[43] In Gaya, officials took the drastic measure of ruling that only women who could "produce a certificate from one of the Indian members of the Committee, stating the applicants are *Pardanashins*" would be admitted to Lady Elgin Zanana (*sic*) Hospital.[44]

While patients brought in by the police were not seeking medical care voluntarily, the question of agency remains for other patients. The only cases Haimabati mentioned were individuals brought to the hospital by their families or employers. But the lady physician in-charge of the Victoria hospital claimed women desired treatment and were prevented from getting it by their husbands. "I have observed that very frequently the husband or the brother of a patient, who would be glad to come as an in-patient, prevent her from remaining, or they take her away as soon as she is admitted,"[45] she wrote in an official report indirectly praising the Raj for trying to save women from the cruelty of their own culture. Without first-hand accounts, it is impossible to know if women wanted to be admitted to these hospitals.

Nor do we know if women made decisions about home treatment. The Dufferin Fund claimed-high caste/upper-class women received Western medical attention only when there were women doctors, or when a third party represented their complaints to male doctors. Culture was to blame and both women and men observed and upheld its dictates. However, autobiographical anecdotes and comments in official reports about Calcutta inform us men of means wanted the most prestigious doctors for their womenfolk. They admired foreign credentials and were willing to call a high-ranking male doctor to treat their wives, daughters, and daughters-in-law within the confines of the home. I do not know if male doctors outside Calcutta treated women in their homes but I expect they were sometimes invited to do so. The presence of women practitioners in the districts made Western medicine available to a significant number of women who could now be treated in their homes or send a proxy to state their problems at the dispensary. However, this did not mean that the decision to consult a doctor or when to consult her were made by women.

Regardless of who called her, when a lady doctor made a home visit the patient had a face-to-face consultation with a woman trained in Western medicine. Campbell doctors were Bengali speakers familiar with local customs and they knew how to use forceps, understood basic hygiene, and could dispense useful medicines. The only story I can relate to suggest how they may have directly benefited women comes from Haimabati's memoir. Soon after arriving in Hooghly, she met a former classmate, a young widow with children, who had remarried. Her classmate confessed she was pregnant at the time of her marriage, and asked Haimabati to be her doctor. Haimabati assented, tacitly agreeing she would deliver a "premature" child. In this case, a woman doctor played an important role in protecting a woman.

What kind of medicine?

A third question that needs to be raised involves the kind of medicine Campbell lady doctors delivered to their patients. I think they practiced medicine differently than either British-trained doctors or Calcutta Medical College graduates because of their cultural background, medical training, and the conditions of their hospitals and dispensaries.

Because they had grown up in Bengal, they knew the language and usually the local dialect where they practiced. Ironically, the Dufferin Fund, which used "the gender-before-race argument," that women had to be treated by women, were not concerned about English women doctors speaking to patients through interpreters.[46] In contrast, Campbell doctors were steeped in "local knowledge," but their medical knowledge was suspect.

The majority of Campbell's students lacked formal education and even those who had gone to school had not studied science. Examination results make it clear they had difficulty mastering the material; after graduation they were professionally isolated. Distance from Calcutta, inferior professional status, and gender conspired to keep them ignorant of new procedures and advances in treatment.

We know very little about how Campbell women practiced medicine in private homes but we can look at hospital records to answer the question of how medicine itself might have been altered by their actions. Surgery is a case in point. It was not common in traditional Indian medical systems, and for reasons associated with rules of purity and pollution, not a desirable procedure. In contrast,

British officials saw surgery as basic to Western medicine and a way to woo "natives" away from traditional systems. In 1894, the Lieutenant-Governor expressed satisfaction that the total number of major and minor operations had increased in a year from 86,915 to 92,476, a net gain of 5,561. Because "the fame and popularity" of government sponsored institutions rested on the success of surgery, officers who performed more than 150 procedures during the year were to be commended. The majority of procedures were to remove cataracts and most were successful. Only a few operations were performed on women but among them were eight ovariotomies, resulting in five deaths.[47] Despite this dismal record, the Lieutenant-Governor hoped to increase the number of female patients.

European women doctors were equally eager to perform surgery but they had difficulty getting patients. Dr. Baümler, in charge of Victoria Hospital, lamented her difficulty finding patients willing to undergo surgery. She blamed the fact that she had performed only 16 procedures on the women themselves. They would agree to minor operations but baulked at the suggestion of a major procedure. Dr. Baümler wrote:

It is ... remarkable how very timid and reluctant patients seem to be, especially in this part of India, to face bodily pain and to submit even to the smallest operation.... In other cases [when] the consent to operate has been given, and just shortly before the operation was to take place the patient is taken away by her relatives or she insists on leaving the hospital for a few days only, on the plea that some near relative is very ill or dying; the faithful promise to return very seldom is kept. [48]

In mofussil hospitals, Civil Surgeons took charge of the major procedures and Campbell graduates assisted. At Hooghly Dufferin Hospital the Civil Surgeon and the Imambara Hospital's doctor outranked the lady doctor and performed major operations. In 1895, Haimabati Sen's second year at Chinsurah, these two men performed 24 major and 77 minor operations in the women's hospital.[49] The next year Haimabati assisted in six procedures—removing placentas and intervening in obstructed labor. In the same year, she used forceps on seven occasions and performed four craniotomies on patients she saw in their homes.[50] By 1897

Dr. Sen was operating alone in the hospital and out-patient clinic: removing retained placentas, turning fetuses in deliveries, opening boils and abscesses, removing warts, extracting teeth, and bandaging simple fractures.[51] After the classification changed in 1900, Dr. Sen performed 10 "major or selected" in-hospital operations while her male colleagues performed 16.[52] Compared to the 150 surgeries per year necessary to win a commendation, these numbers are insignificant. Moreover, about half were for cataracts, the others were obstetrical in nature.[53]

There is a difference in both the number and nature of surgeries performed by Campbell graduates and male doctors. Campbell women performed simple relief-producing procedures, such as tooth extractions, and obstetrical procedures. Although women graduates of Medical College, because they were not directly supervised by the Civil Surgeons, performed a greater number of procedures than Campbell doctors, the list of procedures is similar. European-trained or Medical College-trained male doctors performed more operations than women doctors and appeared to favor experimentation and radical procedures. While women delivered babies with forceps and extracted teeth, male doctors removed uteruses, amputated limbs, performed ovariotomies, and experimented with lithotomy and even clitoridectomies.

There is no simple way to explain this difference. We can assume male doctors accepted an ideology of Western medicine that made them value surgery and experimentation. But I would also suggest that they regarded their Indian female patients as expendable for we find them expressing only disappointment when women refused ovariotomies even when they knew this procedure was almost always fatal. Women doctors, even those with MB and MD degrees, were not part of the male establishment. They could not join the Indian Medical Service, become professors at Medical College, take part in medical conferences, or contribute to scientific journals. I suspect discrimination, rather than enlightened ideas, explains the paucity of spectacular surgeries during their medical careers. Campbell graduates were even more restricted. They were seldom allowed to perform the most prestigious surgical procedures even though the patients were women. It is difficult to determine how they regarded surgery, but we know they performed fewer dangerous procedures and were responsible for fewer fatalities.

One of the ways the cultural sympathies of Campbell graduates found expression was in their view of traditional practitioners and medicine. Hospitals were required to employ compounders, nurses, and midwives but it was difficult to find women trained in these fields. Midwives trained in Eden Hospital and compounders from Campbell were engaged as soon as they graduated. Victoria Hospital could afford a European trained doctor, female compounder, and trained nurses and midwives but this was not the case in mofussil establishments. Inadequate budgets forced these hospitals to make do with apprentice-compounders and *dhais*. Haimabati Sen, who had only Rs 10 a month for the compounder's salary, hired a young man who slept in the hospital. This was a bone of contention with the Civil Surgeons who inspected her hospital and commented time and again on the "irregularity" of the situation.[54] Nor could she afford trained nurses or midwives. In addition to the compounder, Dr. Sen's staff included a male "dresser" (Rs. 5 per month), a *dhai* (Rs. 7 per month), and a sweeper (Rs. 7 per month). For the first few years, the only female employee was the *dhai*, the rest were males. The *dhai* frequently had to assist Dr. Sen or care for patients alone even though her training in Western medicine was limited to what she learned from the lady doctor.

In the eyes of the European medical establishment *dhais* and *kavirajs* [Aryuvedic doctors] were dangerous quacks. The object was to root them out, replace them with medical professionals trained and licensed by British institutions and supervised by officials of the Raj. Dr. Sen has not commented on the *dhais* she worked with, certainly not in the negative fashion that characterized official and missionary literature of the day. Moreover, she wrote of consulting local *kavirajs*, disagreeing with her male supervisors about the wisdom of invasive treatment, and resorting to what sound like traditional folk medicine to treat illnesses: "water with candied sugar and lime," "rice and fish curry." When funds were insufficient to buy foreign-produced medicines, she and other lady doctors purchased traditional remedies in the local bazaar.

CONCLUSIONS

In the late nineteenth century, the colonial government decided to promote Western medical care for Indian women from high-ranking and respectable families. Their efforts were informed by a static view of purdah and a construction of the zenana as a dangerous and unhealthy place where disloyalty flourished and women suffered without medical aid. Their goal was to penetrate the zenana, not with force but with the forceps of the lady doctors. To do so they created a new and inferior class of lady doctors, trained in Western medicine through the vernacular, and supported their employment in women-only hospitals in the districts of Bengal. At the same time, they worked to discredit traditional medicine and medical practitioners.

The Viceroy pronounced the experiment successful, but when we look more closely the picture changes. The women who carried out the medical mission of the Raj were not true believers, partly because of inadequate training, partly because they were trained in and worked in the vernacular. Delivering Western medicine without an adequate support system, they had to rely on traditional practitioners and traditional medical remedies. Practicing medicine in private homes meant they were subject to the rules of these households and had to work in harmony with the beliefs about medicine they found there. What I am suggesting is that Campbell women actually delivered a hybrid form of medicine. Furthermore, we must remember that the women they delivered it to were not passive subjects without cultural systems of their own.

This is a study of interactive adaptation and its essence is not covered in the literature on colonial medicine. Clearly we need to look more carefully at the experience of Western medicine in India to try to understand to what extent medicine itself might have been modified in this process. The interesting questions are about how people responded to this new presence in their midst.

Historiography

The First Step in Writing Women's History
Locating and Preserving Documents

THE BEGINNING

I began my research career in India in 1969 and by 1970, I was hooked on what has become my life's work. Early in 1970, I met Shudha Mazumdar, the great granddaughter of one of the founders of Hindu-Positivism, the subject of my dissertation. Shudha not only helped me with my research, but over tea and biscuits she regaled me with stories of her childhood and years as a child bride.[1] Fascinated by this real-life account of child marriage in the early twentieth century, I asked more questions. One day Shudha casually asked me if I would like to read her memoirs. Her question surprised me. Although her spoken English was excellent, she had less than four years of formal education and I was amazed she had written a book. When Shudha Mazumdar opened her cupboard and handed over a heavy manuscript, she altered the course of my life. I fell in love with the memoirs, and asked her permission to edit them for publication. This practice of following my sources still determines my research agenda three decades later.

Back in the United States, I completed my dissertation, accepted a teaching position, and began my work on these memoirs. Because Shudha had recounted her life in response to questions of friends at different times, the manuscript required extensive editing to produce a chronological narrative. Trying to understand the context of her life, I returned to India to read records of women's

Shudha Mazumdar in riding suit. Darjeeling, c. 1933 (Shudha Mazumdar Collection)

organizations, search archives and libraries, and meet and talk to women active in the social reform and political movements of the first half of the century.

Before I discuss the materials and information I found, I want to address the question of feminist historiography. I first went to India in 1969 when the war in Vietnam, the counter culture, and the women's movement were hot topics on university campuses. Women graduate students were meeting to talk about being taken seriously as professionals. Instead of putting feminism and women's issues on hold, my study of Indian history brought them into sharp relief. The very act of doing research in India presented challenges related to gender and my research led me literally and figuratively to women who were left out of history.

In India I engaged in countless discussions about the value and limitations of feminism for the Indian experience, past and present. These were lively debates, fueled by both the contemporary situation and our reading of the women's movement in India. For example, Sarojini Naidu, doyen of the movement, repeatedly stated "I am not a feminist," and referred to herself as "a mere woman" or "only a woman."[2] In London in 1928, she said she would be ashamed to belong to a feminist movement because feminism seemed to be a "confession of women's inferiority." Then I returned home to find both the Indian women's movement and historians studying it dismissed as irrelevant to serious women's history. Whatever Indian women had done was measured in terms of the suffrage movement or the women's gathering at Seneca Falls, New York in 1848, the first convention on women's rights. The statements of women like Sarojini Naidu were taken at face value and Indian women's delegations to ask for the franchise were not placed within the context of Indian history. Instead, both were judged weak imitations of the protests mounted by their elder and wiser sisters in the United States. Moreover, those of us researching this history were chided for not following in our colleagues' theoretical footsteps.

Many of us found the Western narrative of women's history inadequate as a model for our work and were equally dismayed by the demands of publishers for "juicy" narratives. While editors rejected studies of Indian women based on research, they were happy to publish Mary Daly's *Gyn/Ecology: The Metaethics of Radical Feminism* exposing various forms of "female sacrifice" in India.[3] Daly was a great admirer of Katherine Mayo, the author of *Mother India*. India was backward, Mayo informed the world in 1927, because Hinduism mandated forms of sexuality that rendered its followers weak, cowardly, and incapable of ruling themselves.[4]

Mother India, reprinted several times, found its way into every library in the United States, and by the 1950s was one of the most popular sources for learning about India.[5] It was still being read in the late 1970s when Daly called it an important feminist document and injected new life into Mayo's views. To counter the impact of these popular but flawed accounts, historians realized they would have to rewrite the history of Indian women using solid archival material. However, the first step involved uncovering and preserving these sources.

We have made great strides since the 1970s in preserving sources indispensable for writing the history of Indian women. Much of my work has involved memoirs and photographs, sources that are not part of the conventional archive and that demand new approaches.

MEMOIRS

My luck in finding and then receiving permission to edit memoirs is not easy to explain. I began with Shudha Mazumdar's life story, then worked with Manmohini Zutshi Sahgal, who had written a memoir, and finally with the notebooks Haimabati Sen left with her son. In addition to these three major works, I have written an introduction to the memoirs of Lakshmi Sahgal, Captain Lakshmi of the Indian National Army, and collected short memoirs from a number of women.[6] I am only one of a number of historians who have turned their attention to memoirs and memories in the last two decades.[7] While the total number of these publications is still relatively small, they have added a personal and gendered dimension to our understanding of history.

To illustrate this point, I want to refer to the memoirs of Haimabati Sen, a child widow who later remarried and became the "lady doctor" of Hooghly Dufferin Hospital for Women. When I was first handed Haimabati Sen's notebooks, I had little understanding of medical women's careers in India. I had read about American and European medical women who had gone to India and two famous Indian women doctors: Kadambini Ganguli and Anandabai Joshi, but knew little about medical education for women. The major works on colonial medicine have by and large ignored both women and gender.[8]

In the nineteenth-century Bengal, Indian women were admitted to two kinds of programs in Western medicine: degree programs at Calcutta Medical College, which required a BA for entrance, and vernacular programs taught in medical schools, such as Campbell Medical School, which required only an entrance exam. Haimabati was one of the destitute widows who managed to pass this exam and complete the Vernacular Licentiate in Medicine and

Surgery. She and her colleagues needed to support themselves and found positions in women's hospitals, women's wards of general hospitals, and dispensaries in the districts.

Using the memoir to guide me through conventional archival sources, I was able to flush out the details of their medical training and careers as "lady doctors." Government records, especially reports on education and on government assisted hospitals, included information that could be matched with Haimabati's account and guided me to the education and careers of her and her classmates. Comments in her memoir were equally valuable in leading me to the records of the Dufferin Fund. This "fund" was the National Association for Supplying Female Medical Aid to the Women of India, begun in 1885 by the Countess of Dufferin, to support medical training and care for Indian women. Because Haimabati and many of her friends received Dufferin scholarships and were employed in Dufferin hospitals, the association's records included information about their education, conditions of work, and patients.[9]

The picture that emerges from a joining of the memoir and the archives casts the colonial medical project in a new light. Published sources and archival material portrayed Indian men who completed medical college as true believers in Western science. Although acutely aware of the racism they faced from British professionals, they remained totally devoted to Western medicine and the scientific method. In contrast, those who received the less rigorous vernacular medical training were not completely indoctrinated into the Western system. Because so much of their work was done in dispensaries and private homes instead of hospitals, in a language shared by the doctor and patient, they could not ignore cultural beliefs about diseases and remedies. Although this is not an easy topic to research, studying the kind of medicine these vernacular doctors practiced could help us understand the extent to which medicine itself might have been modified in the colonial context.

PRESERVING MEMOIRS

In addition to an interest in memoirs by publishers such as Kali for Women and Stree, established libraries and new organizations are concerned with their preservation. For example, SPARROW [Sound and Picture Archives for Research on Women] in Mumbai is aggressively collecting women's documents, while older institutions, such as the Centre for Studies in Social Sciences [CSSS] in Kolkata and the Roja Muthiah Research Library [RMRL] in Chennai, have decided to acquire women's records for their larger collections. To date we have only collected a fraction of what actually exists, but the number of young men and women doing research on gender topics makes me hopeful we will uncover more writings by women.

Oral history is another method of preserving women's accounts of their lives. The largest oral history project thus far was that begun by the Nehru Memorial Museum and Library on the freedom struggle that included both men and women. C.S. Lakshmi, the founder of SPARROW, has developed an on-going project to interview and record women who are "makers of history," but have never been the subjects of historical inquiry. In addition to creating tapes for use by future researchers, SPARROW has produced a number of booklets with transcripts of the interviews as well as photographs. The SPARROW series includes booklets such as *Amhihi Itihas Ghadawala* by the Dalit feminist writer Urmila Pawar and *The World as My Laboratory* by scientist Shantoo Gurnani. Since the arts are C.S. Lakshmi's passion, she has included musicians, vocalists, artists, sculptors, and actresses neglected by other historians. The series includes *Pramila* on the Jewish actress Esther Victoria Abraham, and *A Poem Slumbers in My Heart* by the poet Jameela Nishat. In addition to developing a valuable archive, SPARROW is translating these booklets into seven regional languages.[10] These efforts to preserve women's memoirs and memories are all fairly recent and can never recover what has already been lost. While the work of an organization like SPARROW is impressive, they are under-funded and cramped for space. And although other institutions, such as CSSS and RMRL are better funded, collection and preservation of women's memories and documents are not their primary focus.

PHOTOGRAPHS

I first began to look at photographs because people asked me to. Years ago Ralph Nicholas wrote a paper entitled "Listening to What People Tell You: The Cultural Study of Indian Society," urging researchers to listen carefully and be prepared to change their original questions.[11] When I first read this article in the mid-1970s it resonated with my experiences and guided me to listen more carefully to what people were telling me. At that time, I had decided to travel around India to meet women who had played roles in the social reform movement and freedom struggle. When I met them, I asked if they had kept letters, diaries, or journals. Sometimes they showed me letters or organizational documents, but more frequently these women told me their stories. On more than one occasion people offered to show me photographs. I sometimes said "no thanks," or looked at their collections to be polite.

Later, when I began to write, I found myself recalling images that helped explain historical events. For example, I was interested in the effectiveness of women who picketed cloth and liquor

Women demonstrators released from prison. Lahore, 1931 (Manmohini Zutshi Sahgal Collection)

shops. One photo I have, of Lilavati Munshi picketing a foreign cloth shop in Bombay, illustrates why women were successful. In this photo, Lilavati is arguing with four white policemen and they are surrounded by a crowd of Indian men. Seeing one woman in a sea of men underscores the symbolic value of women emerging from "inside" to take part in public demonstrations. I have other photos of women coming out of jail in Lucknow to be felicitated by the crowd, a dramatic comment on public support for their actions. I soon grasped the value of images to supplement written records.

However, I found the archives of libraries, newspapers, and photographic studios disappointing in my search for historical photographs. When I turned to family collections, I discovered that many urban middle-class families documented the lives of their members through photographs. With the help of families in western and eastern India, I collected visual and oral life histories of a number of Indian women, born around 1900. These women related their life histories while we looked at family photographs. Following the session, I copied significant images and developed a method of storing each image with the interviewee's account of what the picture meant. This laborious but exciting method has added new dimensions to my work.

When using photographs as aids to memory, interviewees frequently recalled details they had not previously mentioned and recast their life experiences differently than in written memoirs or formal interviews. In the process of examining my data, I discovered new questions about role conflict, relationships, and presentation of self. Utilizing a combination of photographs and interview questions allows for the emergence of historical evidence not available in the written record.

To illustrate, I will describe a few photographs from the collection of Krishnabai Nimbkar. Born Krishnabai Rau, Krishnabai had an extensive collection of photographs of her natal family, childhood, and youth; her husband's natal family and previous three wives; and their life together. These were carefully stored in trunks and Krishnabai spent hours going through them with me.

Krishnabai Rau was born in Madras in 1906 and first photographed when she was three or four, seated on her father's knee. In the photo are her mother and father and four of their five children. In Madras, her family was part of a tightly knit Maharashtrian community involved in government service. Her father was an employee of the Revenue Department and a Theosophist, while her mother was a reformist Hindu. They welcomed foreign visitors to their home and encouraged debate and discussion of social and political issues.

In her collection are a number of photos of Krishnabai's mother, Kamalabai, both before and after marriage. Kamalabai, married at ten, did not live with her husband until she was fifteen. Tutored in English at home, she became interested in women's rights and by the 1920s, had joined the Women's Indian Association. Kamalabai's oldest daughter, Indirabai, was married at twelve, despite Kamalabai's interest in social reform. The extended family was conservative when it came to marriage and the two eldest daughters were married very young. Family photographs document these marriages.

By the time Krishnabai came of age, her mother was totally opposed to child marriage and in favor of female education. In an interview for the Nehru Library, Krishnabai said: "[My mother] wanted me to grow up and get an education. I had also come to form firm views and opinions on whether I wanted to marry early. I wanted to study more and become something big."[12]

Her father's stroke in 1918 would have put the topic to rest were it not for relatives. When Krishnabai was visiting Bombay, they took her to a studio for a "showing photograph" (*reproduced on page 152*). Then in the ninth standard at school (around twelve or thirteen years of age), she recalled being angry that anyone would suggest marriage when she was intent on studying. However, she had no choice but to comply with their wishes and assume a fashionable pose.

When Krishnabai's father died in 1922, he left his wife with two children to educate and her own ailing mother to care for. They had sold their house but it was still necessary for Kamalabai to work as a matron in a women's home to make ends meet. Although Krishnabai entered Queen Mary's College on a scholarship, family members were still concerned about her

*Krishnabai Rau. Showing
photo, c. 1918 (Krishnabai
Nimbkar Collection)*

marriage. There are very few photographs to document this period
although there is a second "showing photograph" (*reproduced on
page 153*). Krishnabai recalled that this time she had resisted; when
she showed me the photograph she said, "I looked as mean as
possible so that no one would want to marry me."[13] Even though
"the look" is not obvious to the casual viewer, Krishnabai believed
it would deter prospective mothers-in-law.

    While the process of photographing the family and then
arranging their pictures might seem to mimic the imperial project,
or be read as inscribing and reinforcing patriarchy through the
photograph album, I wanted to know the meaning of the
photographs for the subjects themselves. In examining family
photographs with women of this age cohort, I learned that
photographs were not fixed items in terms of historical identity
but rather objects of negotiation between the subject (also the
object of the photograph) and the viewer. I am now interested in
how we can understand and privilege these "tellings" of

*Krishnabai Rau. Second
showing photo, c. 1922–23
(Krishnabai Nimbkar
Collection)*

photographs within larger issues of modernity, the patriarchal
family, and the nation.

PRESERVING PHOTOGRAPHS

What is being done to preserve these valuable sources? This is a
completely new issue in India and the answer right now is "Not
much." Those of us interested in photographs have watched family
collections sold as used paper, seen glass plate negatives for sale in
flea markets, and examined worm-infested images. Some of the
most important collections have been stolen or purchased by
collectors, allowed to rot when buildings were sold, or burned, as
in the case of Bourne and Shepherd.[14] Most archivists complain
they barely have the resources needed to preserve books and
manuscripts and cannot handle photographs. The Nehru Library,
excellent in its other collections, has albums from the freedom
struggle but has made no systematic attempt to collect more

photographs or assemble these for use by readers. Three archives now systematically collect photographs: SPARROW in Mumbai, the CSSS in Kolkata and the Centre for Women's Development Studies in New Delhi.[15] Collecting will be the easier task—at present there are many elderly people anxious to place their collections. However, the preservation of photographs is an extremely difficult task in a country such as India that experiences both high temperatures and high humidity.

CONCLUSIONS

Writing the history of women in India was impossible until we began to search for, unearth, and preserve women's documents. I have been concerned, however, with more than simply writing women's history; I have wanted to put women into history on their own terms.

The dialogue that occurs when I inquire about people's lives and photographs provides the model for what I think feminist history must be. When I work with an individual who is showing me her family collection it becomes a joint project. When examining photographs, I am not the one in control—it is the keeper of the collection who sets the time, place, and pace; determines which photographs I will see, selects the questions she likes and answers them; and decides how the images will be framed. My questions guide and probe but they never dominate—the interviewee is in charge.

In the course of these interviews, I have had to change my questions and invent new ones to keep pace with my subjects. And the exchange does not end with the interview. Many of the women I have met continued to revise their versions of their lives, search for new evidence and information, and add to my collection of data on their lives through letters and conversations. In other words, my project is no longer mine—the subjects have become participants and collaborators. When this collaboration occurs, I feel I am the closest I will ever be to doing feminist women's history.

Reflections on South Asian Women's History

At the first conference held on Women's History in Bangladesh,[1] a member of the audience commented that she and many others had pursued "women's history" long before it had a name. She joked about the term "gender" as another example of innovative renaming and asked what was really new. During the conference, I talked with students enrolled in Dhaka University's Women's Studies program and learned that they regarded women's studies, gender studies, and feminism as one and the same. In their view, focusing on women as a course of study was a political and social act, a statement about their priorities and life choices. The woman who posed the question and the Women's Studies students expressed a deep commitment to changing the reality of women's lives and saw women's history and women's or gender studies as a means to that end.

These experiences are a fitting introduction to this essay in which I reflect on the connection between politics and South Asian women's history, and urge feminist scholars to pay attention to the histories being written and the politics that inform them. As feminists and scholars we recognize that politics play a role in the topics we choose and the way we write, but for those of us who live in the West this means something quite different than it does for our colleagues in India, or Bangladesh, or Pakistan, or Sri Lanka. For us, calling oneself a feminist or deciding to write women's history are personal and professional decisions. They are not, in themselves, political acts with consequences beyond one's social circle and workplace. This essay is not a comprehensive review of women's history[2] but rather an attempt to survey the progress of women's history in India in relation to political events and scholarly trends.

The "woman question" emerged in nineteenth century India as colonial officials, progressives, and traditionalists debated women's relationship to modernity. While a great deal was written about women, there were no histories of women until the 1930s. These first histories, written by men, were based as much on fantasy as research, and usually glorified the ancient past.[3] Neera Desai's *Woman In Modern India* (1957), the first scholarly (and the first feminist) history of Indian women, included a critique of Indian society.[4] In contrast, most of the books about Indian women published in the 1950s and 1960s celebrated their political achievements in the struggle for freedom from British rule.[5] *Towards Equality: the Report of the Committee on the Status of Women In India* (1974) was the next major publication after Desai's to candidly assess the position of women. This report not only influenced how historians would read the history of women from independence until the 1970s, it set the research agenda for the future. From the mid-1970s to the mid-1980s, historians focused on locating and preserving women's records, making women visible, and documenting the lives of non-elite women.

India's first Women's Studies programs, also begun in the 1970s, introduced women as a research subject. *Towards Equality's* argument, that the majority of women did not enjoy "the rights and opportunities guaranteed to them by the Constitution,"[6] injected a note of immediacy into the project. According to Vina Mazumdar, the outspoken Member-Secretary of the Committee, this document set the agenda for emerging Women's Studies programs: to work for policies that would benefit women, convince the social science community to include gender as a category of analysis, and revive the debate on women's issues.[7] The early 1980s witnessed the first national Women's Studies conferences and a host of local, regional, and national meetings focused on specific themes. Fueled by a passion for gender equity and social justice, these programs appealed to a government concerned about women's development. The Sixth Five-Year Plan, 1980–1985, included a chapter on women and development and in 1986 parliament adopted a National Policy on Education that included a section on women's equality that recognized the role Women's Studies could play in transforming society. The University Grants Commission [UGC] then appointed a Standing Committee to introduce Women's Studies centers that would engage in research, teaching, and outreach.[8] By 2003 the number of supported units totaled 34 centers and four cells.

Women's Studies in India has developed differently than Women's Studies in the West. While feminist scholars in American colleges and universities worked to develop undergraduate majors and graduate degrees in Women's Studies within their institutions, research and activism have motivated programs in India. Kumud Sharma observed that although Women's Studies was not yet clearly defined in the early years, those associated with the project wanted to transform traditional disciplines to include women and gender, and affect policy making.[9] There are fewer degree programs in Women's Studies in India than in the USA, but Women's Studies centers have done a great deal to promote the integration of material on women and a gendered worldview into already existing courses and programs.

Women's Studies programs in India maintain a closer association with activism than is generally true in the United States. On the one hand, the UGC mandate required Women's Studies programs to be "instruments of social engineering,"[10] but Women's Studies was also influenced by the women's movement.[11] At the 1996 Berkshire Conference on the History of Women, Tanika Sarkar spoke of the intimate relationship between writing women's history and political activism. Joining protest movements in the 1970s, historians learned about women's condition first-hand, experienced the exhilaration of action, and analyzed female subculture. With the rise of the Hindu right in the 1980s and its manipulation of a gendered narrative, many of these women found themselves engaged in a contest over representation. According to Sarkar, women historians are caught within the dialectics of empowerment and containment.[12] They live in a world where they cannot escape the political and social consequences of their scholarship.

From the late 1980s, these historians turned their attention to metastructures, especially colonialism and its impact on women. The articles published together in Recasting Women, edited by Kumkum Sangari and Sudesh Vaid (1989),[13] reassessing women as a nationalist construction, proved immensely influential in setting the direction of historical inquiry. For example, Partha Chatterjee's essay on the nation and its women, first published in this volume, explains how nationalists fashioned a "new woman" controlled by "new patriarchy."[14] Tanika Sarkar has complicated the discussion of nationalist ideas about women through an examination of debates about social issues and women's and men's writings. In Hindu Wife, Hindu Nation she traces the nationalist construction of women to its final resolution in the safe image of mother and son.[15] Other historians, for example, Sonia Nishat Amin,[16] Swapna Banerjee,[17] and Judith Walsh[18] continue to explore issues of domesticity in the colonial period.

Feminist scholars cheered the advent of Subaltern Studies, the challenge to elitist colonialist, nationalist, and Marxist historiography begun by Ranajit Guha over two decades ago. But the Subaltern Collective neglected women and gender issues until Gayatri Spivak, who defines her field as interventionist cultural studies, joined the group. In "Can the Subaltern Speak?" Spivak addressed the problem of writing the history of colonized women who suffered the oppression of colonialism and patriarchy in their own time, and the oppression of western scholarship as historicized subjects.[19] Historians writing women's/gender history have taken Spivak's charge seriously. For example, Kamala Visweswaran, in her article, "Small Speeches, Subaltern Gender: Nationalist Ideology and Historiography,"[20] suggests it is possible to rescue the female subaltern for history by looking at "the point of erasure."[21] Although the inclusion of women/ gender is now a part of the Subaltern mission, the school's greatest impact on women's history has been through the questions it raised. [22]

This period saw scholars utilize the new historiography to reread and recast existing sources, and examine newly discovered and preserved records. The results were impressive, for example, *Women Writing in India*, edited by Susie Taru and K. Lalita, is a translated and edited collection of women's writing from 600 BCE.[23] Other historians have edited recovered writings for publication. Here I would mention my own work on the memoirs of Shudha Mazumdar, Manmohini Zutshi Sahgal, and Haimabati Sen,[24] Tanika Sarkar's translation and analysis of Rashsundari Devi's memoir,[25] and Rimli Bhattacharya's translation of Binodini Dasi's writings.[26] These works both retrieve women's writings and encourage reflection on issues of agency, victimhood, and cultural differences.

In the 1990s, historians turned their attention to the nation, including an examination of its origins in relation to women and gender. The first feminist explorations of the 1947 Partition were published in *Economic and Political Weekly* in 1993. In an article on the recovery of abducted women, Ritu Menon and Kamla Bhasin argue that the story of 1947 must be

... a gendered narrative of displacement and dispossession, of large-scale and wide-spread communal violence, and of the realignment of community and national identities as people were forced to accommodate the dramatically altered reality that now prevailed. [27]

Urvashi Butalia's *The Other Side of Silence*,[28] among the first gendered monographs on partition, questions historical memory, writing history, and the historian's reliance on archival documents. In this highly personal account, Butalia asks whether a "gendered telling of Partition" exists. In answer to her own question, she discusses the value of feminist historiography, especially to open up new questions, "recover hidden voices," and listen to silence. At the same time, she challenges the simplistic notion that "breaking the silence" is liberating.[29] At present, there are at least three major research projects exploring memories of the partition of Bengal and the Punjab, all sensitive to issues of gender and memory.

The last decade has also been marked by a growing interest in cultural studies, by which I mean interdisciplinary work that borrows from disciplines such as anthropology, gender studies, and literary criticism to challenge the practices, theories, and knowledge of conventional disciplines. Scholars of Indian women's history have found the writings of Edward Said, Michel Foucault, Roland Barthes, Judith Butler, and others instructive in their efforts to rethink the past. For example, Kanchana Natarajan analyzed a Tamil folktale, Sanskrit text, and family structures to demonstrate the relevance of Carroll Smith-Rosenberg's work on women's friendships in nineteenth-century America for understanding social relationships in India.[30] In "Giving Masculinity a History,"[31] Mrinalini Sinha takes Western work on masculinity as the point of departure and reflects on how a history of masculinity that delinks masculinity from maleness would be a significant contribution to both the historiography of colonial India and the study of masculinity. Antoinette Burton has been at the forefront of transnational history, focusing on the complexity and fluidity of colonial encounters in At the Heart of the Empire.[32] Her recently published Dwelling in the Archive addresses two historical issues: the archive and how it is constituted, and Indian women's remembering, in autobiographical works and fiction, of house and home.[33] The three women featured in this monograph share a preoccupation with space, specifically the home, which leads to reflection on identity, nation, and modernity. Burton analyzes how they "used domestic space as an archival source from which to construct their own histories."[34] Cultural Studies have not been separate from other schools of Indian women's history, rather a running dialogue exists between those labeled Subaltern, Marxist, or liberal feminist historians, and those in cultural studies. Their work has played an important role in the development of women's history in India by introducing new theoretical perspectives and approaches.

The attack on the Babri Masjid at Ayodhya in 1992, followed by some of the worst riots in post-independence India, challenged feminist scholars in new ways. Research and writing about women, as well as the feminist movement, had aimed at inclusivity—especially of non-elite women and women from minority communities. There have been challenges to this model since the 1980s, from those who argued feminism was essentially divisive for minority and/or poor communities, and from Hindutva organizations that began to appropriate feminist rhetoric and champion women's rights.[35] In Bombay, the Shiv Sena gained a following among lower middle-class women who appreciated the party's support for daycare centers and microlending schemes, and in turn, accepted new roles as "Durgas" poised to rid the country of evil Muslims. The question for feminists, according to Flavia Agnes, had been whether or not they should work with communal parties when they agreed on issues, or hold fast to a secular ideology. All this changed with the attack on the Babri Masjid and subsequent riots. Agnes writes:

The riots dealt a severe blow to the premise that the women have a separate existence away from their communal identity where they can discuss problems of rape, divorce, maintenance on a common platform. The same issues affect different women in different ways at different times.[36]

She maintains that feminist activists, if they want to change the reality of women's lives in post-Ayodhya India, will have to re-examine women's issues "within the newer challenges to democracy, secularism, and minority rights."[37] These events also touched feminist historians who began to analyze the relationship between "fundamentalism" and "Communalism,"[38] and Hindutva's origins in nineteenth-century nationalist ideas.[39]

The power of communal parties was demonstrated in Gujarat in 2002. In February, Muslims were blamed for attacking and burning a train whose passengers had gone to Ayodhya to celebrate the destruction of the Babri Masjid. Reprisal killings of Muslims began the day after the train was burned. About these incidents Amitav Ghosh wrote:

In the aftermath of the slaughter it has become clear that the machinery of state and possibly even the financial apparatus of the commercial world were bent to the task of instigating and supporting mob violence. In other words, two of the most important forces of order in society were turned to exactly the opposite purpose: undermining peace and promoting violence.[40]

Muslim women, although never accused of burning the train, were deliberately targeted in these incidents of "ethnic cleansing." The reaction of feminist scholars was immediate and their articles condemning these revenge killings were carried in periodicals such as *Manushi, Outlook,* and *Economic and Political Weekly.* Writing on the "Semiotics of Terror," Tanika Sarkar summed up the violence against women:

One can go on narrating the ways in which babies and women were tortured and killed, but the point here is often the two acts were coupled together. The pattern of cruelty suggests three things. One, the woman's body was a site of almost inexhaustible violence, with infinitely plural and innovative forms of torture. Second, their sexual and reproductive organs were attacked with a special savagery. Third, their children, born and unborn, shared the attacks and were killed before their eyes.[41]

This was able to happen, Sarkar argues, because the state had successfully inserted its communal and masculinist agenda into a wide range of public institutions from schools to the police.

Women's Studies programs have been affected by these and other political events and responded with research and programs. To illustrate this I will comment on only two of a number of initiatives: Jadavpur University's "Refresher Courses" in Women's Studies, and Stri Abhyas Shreni [Women's Studies series], a series of basic Women's Studies texts conceived and edited by Neera Desai and Usha Thakkar.

Refresher courses are designed for university and college teachers who need to learn about new developments in the field. Jadavpur University in Kolkata has offered refresher courses in Women's Studies since 1998 and history played a major role in each. The three-week workshops are designed to facilitate the incorporation of Women's Studies issues into existing curricula, make participants aware of the reality of women's lives, teach them how to read texts with a critical eye, and privilege "Third World [women's] experiences" over the Western women's movement. Course designers have been frank about their political aim: to develop teacher-researchers who can "recast or re-create" social reality "in more favorable terms."[42] Women's history has been prominent in these projects and feminist historians such as Tanika Sarkar and Vina Mazumdar presented lectures on the historical and social construction of gender, the role of women in radical movements, and international feminism.

Stri Abhyas Shreni began with a workshop held at SNDT Women's University in the mid-1990s to talk about the availability of Women's Studies literature in regional languages. The participants, all connected with Women's Studies programs, decided to produce a series of short books, written in straightforward, college-level Gujarati for students and teachers of Women's Studies and individuals working with NGOs. The translated titles of these books are descriptive, for example, the first four included *Women's Studies: Expanding Horizons of Knowledge*; *Women and Development*; *Women and Politics: Uphill Task*; and the *Women's Movement: From Equality to Liberation*.[43] The history included in these texts, the editors decided, should be the history of common women, and where there were few records, authors were asked to raise questions about women's role in history and history as a discipline.[44]

The import of the series can be gleaned by looking at two books: *The Women's Movement* by Neera Desai and Tripti Shah, and *Women's Studies* by Neera Desai. *The Women's Movement* begins with the "woman question" in the nineteenth century and traces women's issues from the 1870s through the liberal women's movement in the 1930s to the present. The authors have recognized the significance of nineteenth-century reform movements and Gandhi in improving women's position, connected the women's movement to political movements, and acknowledged the role of international feminism. In *Women's Studies*, Desai critiques histories that simply celebrate women's participation in public life and praises research that explains how gender ideology is maintained and reproduced. While appreciating the contributions of new theoretical approaches, she noted that focusing exclusively on female agency can obscure the role of men in setting the parameters for women's action. Desai worries that in taking difference as the point of departure, we will overlook issues and circumstances where women have worked together to combat oppression.

Towards Equality argued for the inclusion of all women—from minority communities, marginalized groups, and the lower socio-economic strata—in the nation's progress and its history. Studies of women's status and economic needs have been more attentive to these differences than have those by historians. For example, my *Women in Modern India*, which drew on the published literature, does not do justice to the history of Muslim women, Christian women, and women from other minority communities nor to Dalit or tribal women. Historians have only begun to write the history of Muslim women in South Asia. Shahida Lateef's *Muslim Women in India* (1990), Zoya Hasan's edited *Forging Identities* (1994), and Azra Asghar Ali's *The Emergence of Feminism Among Indian Muslim Women, 1920–1947* focus on women's entry into public life and introduce key questions for Muslim women's history.[45] Sonia Nishat Amin's *The World of Muslim Women in Colonial Bengal: 1876–1939*, and Gail Minault's *Secluded Scholars: Women's Education and Muslim Social Reform in Colonial India* are comprehensive works on Muslim women's education, family life, and literary activity in colonial Bengal, and north India respectively.[46] Although the chronicles inform us that Muslim women played important political roles, only a few historians have written about powerful women: Ellison Findley on Nur Jahan, and Shaharyar M. Khan and Claudia Preckel on the Begums of Bhopal.[47] Barbara Metcalf's *Perfecting Women*,[48] a partial translation and commentary of an important document for reformist Islam, and Syeda Saiyidain Hameed's *Hali's Musaddas*[49] on the rise and fall of Islamic civilization by "Urdu's first feminist poet" are of value to feminist historians. Current research, for example that of Siobhan Lambert-Hurley,[50] promises more analysis of powerful women, while Ph.D. candidate Bilkis Rahman mines the archives for documents such as the memoir of Bibi Kusum, the second wife of the renowned novelist Mir Musharraf Hussain.[51] The work of these young historians is encouraging but there is still much to be done. In addition to retrieval projects, to collect and archive writings, memoirs, letters and diaries, photographs, and oral histories of Muslim women, we need to know more about women's response to modernizing trends and efforts to change their lives. I would like to see a study that traces the response of Muslim women to feminist ideas and their adaptation of these ideas so that we could imagine a history of women that was cognizant of difference.

Most of the women now included in history are Hindu, upper caste, and upper class. There has been some attention, but not nearly enough, to non-elite women and regional patterns. There are a few histories of women in pre-independence radical movements, for example, '*We were making history* …' about the Telengana movement, and Peter Custers' *Women in the Tebhaga Uprising.* Dalit women have been discussed in relation to male reformers, especially Phule and Ambedkar, but are only now being addressed as a separate group needing a history.[52] Anupama Rao's *Gender and Caste: Contemporary Issues in Indian Feminism*[53] and forthcoming monograph, *The Caste Question: Untouchable Struggles for Civil Rights and Recognition*, with books such as *The Silken Swing: The Cultural Universe of Dalit Women*[54] are a step in the right direction. I have commented specifically on the need for more attention to the history of Dalit women and Muslim women, but the same is true for tribal women, and women in other religious communities. This project is designed not to support those who would divide women, but to write a more inclusive history that is honest about differences and conflicts over these differences.

Just as the story of Hindu women has often been told as the story of Indian women, so the experiences of Bengali women during the colonial period have been glossed as the experiences of Indian women. Recently published books and research in progress promises to correct the balance. Srimati Basu's *She Comes to Take Her Rights* and Veena Talwar Oldenburg's *Dowry Murder* explore the social consequences of property and property rights for women in North India.[55] Anshu Malhotra's rich monograph, *Gender, Caste, and Religious Identities*, and articles on late nineteenth and early twentieth-century colonial Punjab trace changes in women's status as the new middle-class, high caste elite redefined themselves.[56] Working on western India are Padma Anagol, who writes about gender and reform[57] and is currently engaged in a project on "Indian Women and the Nationalist Movement in Karnataka, *c.* 1880–1947," and Shefali Chandra whose work explores the changing meaning given to English and the vernacular in women's education from the mid-nineteenth century until independence.[58] Barbara Ramusack's current work on the origins and development of maternal and child welfare programs in India compares princely states with British India, extending women's/gender history to a neglected topic in neglected regions.

Historians and archivists are attempting to redefine the archive at the same time they work to preserve women's records.[59] While at first glance this work may seem less connected to politics than writing history or developing Women's Studies programs, this is not the case. To illustrate this point I will comment on C.S. Lakshmi's creation of the archive named SPARROW.

C.S. Lakshmi is the founder of SPARROW, a dynamic organization located in Mumbai. In the late 1980s feminist scholars began talking about the need for a specialized archive for women that would collect materials and at the same time become "an agent of conscientisation."[60] SPARROW's plan from the beginning was to acquire everything from women's private papers and journals to photographs and recordings, and conduct oral history workshops.

SPARROW's oral history project targets women who have been part of history but never before the subjects of historical inquiry. The interviews are recorded during workshops with students, then transcribed and published with photographs in the SPARROW series. It is a project, Lakshmi explained "conceived not only as voicing silence but as one that would lead to communication, sharing and interaction."[61] In choosing as subjects women of different castes and communities, and in responding to the violence of Ayodhya and subsequent riots by organizing a workshop on Communalism, Violence and Women,[62] SPARROW takes a political stand.

CONCLUSIONS

Historians living in India, England, Europe and the USA who study and write about women and gender in India meet in archives and at conferences and read each other's publications. The result has been an impressive exchange of information and a few collaborative projects, but it has not produced an awareness of and/or sensitivity to the context of knowledge production in India.

What do I think we need to take note of? First, there is a pronounced difference in access to resources. While historians in the West are accustomed to using archives on three continents, ordering microfilm and microfiche documents, and downloading articles from electronic databases, only a few historians living in India are able to travel extensively, even in their own country. Books and journals published outside the country are often prohibitively expensive, libraries inadequate, and electronic databases unavailable. Indian colleagues have been creative in their selection and adaptation of Western theoretical works, but the majority of graduate students in Indian universities do not have access to basic texts on theory or Indian women's history. Two publishing ventures address this problem. Stree, a feminist publisher located in Kolkata, has launched a series for students titled "Theorising Feminism," described as "handbooks in the basic concepts of feminism." And, Kali for Women, India's first feminist publishing firm, has selected scholars to develop a "Debates in Indian Feminism" series on topics such as caste, work, dowry, and the media. These are admirable interventions, but Indian faculty and students working on women's/gender history need better stocked libraries, access to databases, as well as research fellowships and travel grants.

Second, we need to rethink the colonial periodization of Indian history into ancient, medieval, and modern, which has been uncritically accepted by many writing women's history. Within this framework, ancient India has been studied to shed light on contemporary views, the fifth to the nineteenth century has been ignored, while "the nation" dominates the modern period. Whether it is colonialism engendered and revisited, or partition, or communalism, the leading questions are about the nation. But this is more than an issue of periodization or focus. History has become a battleground over political ideology. Communalism thrives in an environment where the "Golden Age" of Hinduism (and of women) was brought to an end by "Muslim invasions." By accepting conventional periodization, we miss the point that women's lives are not determined solely by political events and ignore important continuities and discontinuities.

Third, we must transform the definition of sources, the process of archivization, and the assumptions of history to include women and gender. While those writing the history of Indian women are part of the larger historical project (to write the nation), they are only marginally involved in writing the metanarrative. If we review the schools of history in India—colonial, national, Cambridge, and Subaltern—none has existed separate from politics and none has been friendly to a feminist perspective. In terms of their narratives, expectations, and procedures, these schools have little to offer the women's history project, which leads one to wonder if there could be a disciplinary perspective separate from the political.[63] We might look to Women's Studies, where the approaches, questions, and theory seem right, for a disciplinary perspective but Women's Studies is only beginning to address colonialism and international power politics.

Our most important task is to pay attention to the political and economic environment in which feminist scholarship is produced. Three recent publications have focused attention on what scholars have called the "formidable challenges before the women's movement and Women's Studies."[64] When the UGC announced its plan to rename Women's Studies as "Women and Family Studies," it added a new threat to a community already burdened with problems over funding, university structures, research agendas, and the political environment.[65] Among the list of problems facing Women's Studies and the women's movement, Maitreyi Krishnaraj includes Hindutva, the "myth" of empowerment, the "NGO-isation" of women's issues, and the impact of economic reforms. At the same time, she critiques the women's movement for its reliance on legal remedies, and Women's Studies for its shift,

from grappling conceptually and empirically with contemporary development issues and feminist struggles to moving increasingly to 'representation' and post modernist analysis of historical or contemporary texts on media representation.[66]

Like Sumit Sarkar, she would see the challenges facing historians as twofold: from the political system which would use history for its own ends and from new disciplinary imperatives.

As scholars we need to be attentive to the impact of both international and domestic politics on Indian affairs and especially women's issues, and what these mean for those engaged in writing women's/gender history. Recognizing that certain theoretical positions might reduce women's oppression to a discourse to be analyzed, Spivak warned scholars against taking "Foucault and Derrida's side *against* feminists who work on the ground."[67] As feminists we need to be aware that feminism, as Burton writes, "is as much about power as women's rights." In the same sense, women's/gender history that fails to analyze what feminism means to Dalit women, Muslim women, and others, may support the privileged few and keep others in their place. These are the challenges we must take seriously if we are to write the history of women and gender in South Asia and keep feminism relevant in the twenty-first century.

End Notes

INTRODUCTION

1. Mary R. Beard, *Woman as Force in History; a Study in Traditions and Realities* (New York: The Macmillan Company, 1946).
2. Gerda Lerner, *Women in American History* (Menloe Park, CA.: Addison-Wesley, 1971).

CHAPTER 1: CAGED TIGERS

1. Purdah, the English spelling of *parda,* literally means veil or curtain. The term refers to both the curtain used to hide women from outsiders and to a system of seclusion, including veiling, staying within secluded areas, and avoiding contact with unrelated men, practiced differently by Hindus and Muslims.
2. Miriam Schneir, *Feminism: the Essential Historical Writings* (New York: Vintage, 1972), p. xiv.
3. J.A. Banks and Olive Banks, *Feminism and Family Planning in Victorian England* (New York: Schocken, 1964), p. 8.
4. Kate Millett, *Sexual Politics* (New York: Avon, 1971), p. 64.
5. Sylvia Vatuk, "Authority, power and autonomy in the life cycle of the North Indian woman." Paper presented to Association for Asian Studies, Toronto (Mar, 1981). Published as "Authority, Power and Autonomy in the Life Cycle of the North Indian Woman," in *Dimensions of Social Life: Essays in Honor of David G. Mandelbaum*, ed. P. Hockings (Berlin: Mouton de Gruyter, 1987).

6. Raja Rammohun Roy, "Translation of a conference between an advocate for and opponent of the practice of burning widows alive, from the original Bungla (*sic*) (Nov, 1818)," *Social and Educational Works*. 2nd Edn. (Calcutta: np, nd.), pp. 25–53.

7. Sunil Kumar Bose, *Ishwar Chandra Vidyasagar* (New Delhi: National Book Trust, 1969), p. 46.

8. Lotika Ghosh, "Social and educational movements for women and by women, 1820–1950," in *Bethune School and College Centenary Volume, 1849–1949*, ed. Kalidas Nag (Calcutta: Bethune College and School, 1950), pp. 32–33.

9. Gulam Murshid, "Unlatching the cage: male efforts to free Bengali women and women's concept of freedom, 1949–1905." Unpublished paper from author.

10. Elizabeth Cady Stanton (1815–1902) is considered the major architect of the first convention on women's rights, held in Seneca Falls, New York, in 1848. For the next half century, she was a leader of the movement for women's rights in the United States.

11. *The Indian Ladies Magazine* (Feb, 1904), p. 259.

12. *The Indian Ladies Magazine* (Jan, 1905), pp. 219–20.

13. *The Indian Ladies Magazine* (Jan, 1906), pp. 230–32; (Apr, 1907), p. 380; (January, 1908), pp. 227–28.

14. *The Indian Social Reformer* (Aug, 1901), p. 396.

15. Saraladevi, "A Women's Movement," *The Modern Review*, 10 (Oct, 1911), pp. 344–50.

16. *New India* (May 10, 1917), p. 9.

17. Kamalabai L. Rau, *Memoirs of a Brihan Maharashtrian*, trans. Indirabai M. Rau, Unpublished manuscript. (1972), p. 14. This was later published as *Smrutika: The Story of My Mother as Told by Herself* (Pune: Dr. Krishabai Nimbkar, 1988).

18. Rau, pp. 15–18.

19. Geraldine Forbes, "Votes for women: the demand for women's franchise in India, 1917–1937," in *Symbols of Power: Studies on the Political Status of Women in India*, ed. Vina Mazumdar (New Delhi: Allied Publishers, 1979), pp. 3–12.

20. Sarojini Naidu, *Roshni*, 9 (New Delhi, 1957), p. 4.

21. Sarojini Naidu, "Advice to City Fathers of Karachi," *Forward* (Aug 16, 1925), p. 15.

22. Manmohan Kaur, *The Role of Women in the Freedom Movement, 1857–1947* (Delhi: Sterling: 1968), p. 175.
23. All India Women's Conference [AIWC] Report (1928), pp. 37, 40; (1928–29), p. 6.
24. AIWC Report (1928–29), p. 65; Women's Indian Association [WIA] Report (1930–31): Appendix D; Rau, pp. 16–17.
25. Geraldine Forbes, "Women and modernity: the issue of child marriage in India," *Women's Studies International Quarterly.* 2(4) (1979), pp. 407–19; Barbara N. Ramusack, "Women's organizations and social change: the age-of-marriage issue in India," in *Women and World Change: Equity Issues in Development,* ed. Naomi Black and Ann Cottrell (Beverly Hills: Sage, 1981).
26. Burqa, also spelled burka, refers to the enveloping cloak worn in public by Muslim women.
27. Shudha Mazumdar, *A Pattern of Life: The Memoirs of an Indian Woman,* ed. Geraldine Forbes (New Delhi: Manohar, 1977), p. 167.
28. Nehru Memorial Museum and Library (NMML), Muthulakshmi Reddi, in Reddi Papers, nd. File 11.
29. Klash Sobha, "Indian Women Yesterday and Today," *Roshni* (Dec 2, 1947), p. 4.
30. *WIA Report* (1928–1929), 3; Jana Everett, "The Indian Women's Movement in Comparative Perspective" Ph.D. Dissertation (University of Michigan Dissertation, 1976), Chapter VIII. This was published as *Women and Social Change in India* (New Delhi: Heritage, 1979).
31. AIWC Report (1944–1945).
32. AIWC Files. File #314. nd.
33. Evelyn C. Gedge and Mithan Choksi, ed. *Women in Modern India* (Bombay: D. B. Taraporewalla, 1929), p. 10.
34. NMML, Kamaladevi Chattopadhyay to Jawaharlal Nehru. G. 48.1936. Nehru Papers, 1936.
35. Helena Dutt, at an interview with members of Jatiya Mahila Sanghati, Calcutta, Sep 25, 1975.
36. Grace Thompson Seton, *"Yes Lady Saheb": A Woman's Adventurings with Mysterious India* (New York: Harper and Row, 1925), p. 221.
37. Susan S. Wadley, ed. *The Powers of Tamil Women* (Syracuse: Syracuse University Foreign and Comparative Studies, 1980), p. ix.

CHAPTER 2: THE POLITICS OF RESPECTABILITY

1. Gordon Johnson, *Provincial Politics and Indian Nationalism: Bombay and the Indian National Congress, 1880–1915* (London: Cambridge University Press, 1973).

2. For example, see Tara Ali Baig, *India's Women Power* (New Delhi: S. Chand and Co., 1976) and Radha Krishna Sharma, *Nationalism, Social Reform and Indian Women* (Patna: Janaki Prakashan, 1981).

3. For example, see Vijay Agnew, *Elite Women in Indian Politics* (New Delhi: Vikas, 1979) and Gail Pearson, "Women in Public Life in Bombay City with Special Reference to the Civil Disobedience Movement," Ph.D. Thesis, JNU Centre for Historical Studies, 1979.

4. Aparna Basu, "The Role of Women in the Indian Struggle for Freedom," in *Indian Women: From Purdah to Modernity*, ed. B.R. Nanda, (New Delhi: Vikas, 1976), p. 17.

5. Bimanbehari Majumdar and Bhakat Prasad Mazumdar, *Congress and Congressmen in the pre-Gandhian Era, 1885–1917* (Calcutta: Firma K.L. Mukhopadhyay, 1967), pp. 128–29. Majumdar and Mazumdar refer to the two ladies using their husbands' names: Mrs. Ramanibhai Mahipatram, BA (Lady Nilkanth) and Mrs. Sumant Batukram, BA (Sharada Mehta). The Congress anthem listed in the report of 1902 did not have an author. However, it was very similar to a Bengali song composed by Satyendranath Tagore to be sung at the Hindu Mela in Calcutta in 1868. Also see A.M. Zaidi and S. Zaidi, ed. *The Encyclopedia of the Indian National Congress* 4: 1901–1905 (New Delhi: S. Chand and Co., 1978), p. 320.

6. J.C. Bagal, *Jattiya Andolane Bangla Nari* (Calcutta: Vishva-Bharati, Bhadra 1361 B.S. [1954]), p. 15.

7. *The Indian Social Reformer* [*ISR*], (Jun 4, 1899), p. 310.

8. Sumit Sarkar, *The Swadeshi Movement in Bengal, 1903–1908* (New Delhi: People's Pub. House 1973), p. 253.

9. The various notes on women's participation come from J.C. Bagal.

10. From Ramendra Sundar Trivedi's "Banga Lakshsmir Bratakatha," in *Ramendra Rachana Sangraha*, selected and edited by Suniti Kumar Chattopadhyaya (Calcutta: Bangiya Sahitiya Parisad, 1371). Translated by Tridib Ghosh.

11. Ibid.
12. Shudha Mazumdar, *A Pattern of Life, the Memoirs of an Indian Woman*, ed. Geraldine Forbes (New Delhi: Manohar, 1977), p. 58.
13. Bagal, p. 15.
14. Bagal, pp. 15–16.
15. Valentine Chirol, *Indian Unrest* (London: Macmillan and Co., 1910), p. 103.
16. See Veena T. Oldenburg, *The Making of Colonial Lucknow, 1856–1877* (Princeton: Princeton University Press, 1984).
17. Dadabhai Naoroji (1825–1917), the son of a Parsi priest, was the first Indian elected to the British Parliament (1892) and three times President of the Indian National (1886, 1893, 1906). His book, *Poverty and Un-British Rule in India* (1901), explained the imperial drain on Indian finances. A nationalist and social reformer, he was a mentor to men such as M.K. Gandhi.
18. Cambridge University Transcripts, Goshiben Captain, S-22, (16–5–1970); Oriental and India Office Collection [OIOC], Political Dept. B Proceedings, Home Dept. 1913, "History Sheet on Madame Cama," prepared by the Criminal Intelligence Office, Confidential, August 1913, no. 61.
19. Annie Besant, "The Political Status of Women, " Pamphlet, 2nd. Edn. (London: C. Watts, 1885).
20. *ISR* (Mar 17, 1901).
21. "Mrs. Besant on Indian Womanhood," *Indian Ladies Magazine* [*ILM*], 1:7 (Jan, 1902), pp. 195–57.
22. "Mrs. Besant on Womanhood," *ISR* (Mar 17 1901).
23. Arthur H. Nethercot, *The Last Four Lives of Annie Besant* (Chicago: University of Chicago Press, 1963), pp. 232–72; "Annie Besant," *Dictionary of National Biography* [*DNB*], (Calcutta: Institute of Historical Studies, 1972) India, 1, pp. 151–54.
24. "Sarojini Naidu," *DNB* (1974), 3, pp. 194–97; V.S. Naravane, *Sarojini Naidu* (New Delhi: 1980), pp. 15–19; P.A. Subrahmanya Ayyar, *Sarojini Naidu* (Madras: Cultural Books, 1957), p. 221.
25. Gopal Krishna Gokhale (1866–1915) was a prominent social reformer and nationalist from Maharashtra who founded the Servants of India Society, an organization of volunteers dedicated to the social, political, and economic welfare of India. A moderate in politics, Gokhale believed in non-violent cooperation to secure rights.

26. Dhondo Keshav Karve (1858–1962) was a social reformer who devoted his life to the uplift of Hindu widows. In 1895 he began a widow's home in Pune, which was shifted to Hingne in 1900. He added the Mahila Vidyalaya [Women's School] in 1907, another institution to train workers for this school in 1908, and in 1916 founded India's first women's university (later moved to Bombay and renamed SNDT Women's University).

27. "Mrs. Sarojini Naidu," *Forward*, Congress Number (1925): p. 9; "Sarojini Naidu," *DNB*, pp. 194–97; Naravane, Sarojini Naidu Exhibit, Delhi Archives (Dec, 1980).

28. Naravane, *Sarojini Naidu*, pp. 28–31.

29. Dr. Sitaramayya Pattabhi, *The History of the Indian National Congress*, 1, (1885–1935) (Bombay: Padma Publications Ltd., 1935) Reprint 1946, p. 52.

30. A.L. Basham, "Traditional Influences on the Thought of Mahatma Gandhi," in *Essays on Gandhian Politics*, ed. R. Kumar, (Oxford: Clarendon Press, 1971), pp. 26–41. For an excellent article on Gandhi see Madhu Kishwar, "Gandhi on Women," *Economic and Political Weekly*, 20:40 (Oct 5, 1985), pp. 1691–1701 and 20:41 (Oct 12, 1985), pp. 1753–57.

31. Quoted in James D. Hunt's "Suffragettes and Satyagraha: Gandhi and the British Women's Suffrage Movement," presented at the Annual Meeting of the American Academy of Religion, St. Louis, Missouri, Oct, 1976.

32. The Bhagini Samaj [literally, female tigers' association] was founded on Feb 19, 1916 in memory of the late Shri Gopal Krishna Gokhale by his disciple, Shri Karsondas Chitalia, a member of the Servants of India Society. The first president was Smt Jaijee Petit, a Parsi, who was assisted in the early organization by another well-known social worker of Bombay, Lady Lakshmibai Jagmohandas. From *Bhagini Samaj*, a pamphlet (Bombay, nd).

33. Interview with Jaisree Raiji, Bombay, May 2, 1976; M.K. Gandhi, *Women and Social Injustice* (Ahmedabad: Navajivan Publishing House, 1942) 4th Edn., 1954, pp. 4–5.

34. Barbara Southard, "The Feminism of Mahatma Gandhi," *Gandhi Marg*, 3: 7 (Oct, 1981), pp. 404–21.

35. M.K. Gandhi, "Speech at Ladies Protest Meeting, Bombay," *Collected Works of Mahatma Gandhi* [*CWMG*], 15, p. 89.

36. Gandhi, "Speech at Women's Meeting, Godhra," *CWMG*, 16, p. 168; "Speech at Women's Meeting, Dohad," *CWMG*, 16, pp. 79–80; "Speech at Women's Meeting, Rajket," *CWMG*, 16, p. 168; "Speech at Women's Meeting, Surat," *CWMG*, 15, pp. 322–26; "Speech at Women's Meeting, Bombay, *CWMG*, 15, pp. 290–92.

37. "Duty of Women," *CWMG*, 18, pp. 57–58; "Speech at Women's Meeting, Dakor," *CWMG*, 18, pp. 391–95.

38. Articles in *Young India* (Dec 15, 1921), in Gandhi, *Women and Social Injustice*, p. 155; "Women of Gujarat," *CWMG*, 22, pp. 181–82.

39. Shaukat Ali (1873–1938) was born in the princely state of Rampur, studied at Aligarh, and served in the UP civil service from 1896–1913. Jailed from 1915–19 for his political activities against the British for their war against the Ottoman Empire, he was elected president of the first Khilafat conference in 1919. After his release, he became a prominent freedom-fighter and worked with Gandhi and Congress to unite Hindus and Muslims against the British.

40. "Speech at Women's Meeting, Patna," *CWMG*, 19, pp. 67–86.

41. "Speech at Meeting of Muslim Women," *CWMG*, 20, p. 397.

42. Interview with S. Ambujammal, Madras (Jan 19, 1976).

43. "Smt. Sucheta Kripalani," Nehru Memorial Museum and Library (NMML), Oral History Transcript.

44. Pearson, "Women in Public Life," pp. 175–84.

45. *The Indian Annual Register (IAR)*, II (1922), p. 320.

46. *IAR*, I (1922), pp. 44–45.

47. M.K. Gandhi, "Women's Part," *Young India* (Dec 15, 1921).

48. Gail Minault, "Purdah Politics: The Role of Muslim Women in Indian Nationalism, 1911–1924," in *Separate Worlds, Studies of Purdah in South Asia*, eds. Gail Minault and Hanna Papanek (Columbia, Mo: South Asia Books, 1982), p. 254; *IAR*, I (1922), p. 454.

49. *IAR*, I (1922), p. 55.

50. C.S. Lakshmi, *The Face Behind the Mask: Women in Tamil Literature* (Delhi: Vikas, 1984), p. 8.

51. Gandhi, "Fallen Sisters," *CWMG*, 21, pp. 92–95.

52. Gandhi, "Reply to Women's Address, Noakali," *CWMG*, 27, p. 999. Madhu Kishwar argues that Sita and Draupadi were symbols that Gandhi "overburdened" with the qualities he wished them to carry. Kishwar, "Gandhi on Women," *EPW*, 20:40, p. 1691.

53. For a discussion of this topic see Pearson, "Women in Public Life."

54. "Awakened Womanhood of India," *Bombay Chronicle* [BC] (Jul 23, 1930); Booklet from Gandhi Seva Sena, Bombay (cover page missing), pp. 1–3.

55. "Victory or Death Must be Woman's Slogan in the Fight," *BC* (Mar 17, 1931).

56. "Women Satyagrahis," *BC* (Mar 11, 1930); "Dadabhai Naroji's Granddaughter Pleads with Mahatma," *BC* (Nov 31, 1930), p. 1.

57. Agnew, *Elite Women*, p. 39; OIOC, Home Political Dept., 247/II/1930, Reports II, Bombay, Secret-camp Jalalpur (Apr 11, 1931).

58. OIOC, Home Political Dept., 247/II/1930, Reports II, Bombay, Secret and Confidential Reports from Gandhi's March.

59. This program had already been published in *Young India* entitled "To the Women of India." In it Gandhi told women to take up two tasks: boycotting and spinning. He said men could join women in these activities but, since women would run the show, men would be subordinate. "Women's Part in National Struggle," *BC* (Apr 10, 1930), p. 1.

60. "Speech at Gujarati Women's Conference, Dandi, *CWMG*, 43, pp. 251–52; "Special Task Before Women," *CWMG*, 43, pp. 271–75.

61. Gandhi, "How to Do the Picketing," *Young India* (Apr 24, 1930), p. 144.

62. *BC* (Apr 14, 1930).

63. "Women Picket Liquor Shops in Surat," *BC* (Apr 16, 1930), p. 1; "Gandhiji Confers with Women," *BC* (Apr 17, 1930), p. 1; "Women's Response," *BC* (Apr 17, 1930); "Gandhiji Confers with Women on Picketing," *BC* (Apr 18, 1930), p. 1.

64. "Satyagraha Activities in Bombay," *BC* (Apr 30, 1930), p. 1.

65. "Awakened Womanhood of India," *BC* (Jul 23, 1930); Booklet from Gandhi Seva Sangh, p. 5.

66. Nehru Memorial Museum and Library [NMML], All-India Congress Committee [AICC] Files, G-8/1929, Appendix 6, The Constitution of the Desh Sevika Sangh as amended in May, 1931, Captain, Interview.

67. Captain, Interview.

68. Kamaladevi Chattopadhyay, "The Struggle for Freedom," *Women's Forum*, 4 (Jul–Aug 1972).

69. Booklet from Gandhi Seva Sena, p. 7.

70. "Bombay Celebrates Gandhi Birthday," *BC* (Oct 4, 1930), p. 1; "Women's Activities in G Ward," *BC* (Jul 1, 1930); "Desh Sevika Sangh," *BC* (Jul 2, 1930), p. 1; "Women Picketers Bar Voters Way to Polling Booth," *BC* (Sep 19, 1930).

71. "Women Must Share Sacrifice with Men," *BC* (May 15, 1930), p. 1.

72. Captain, Interview.

73. NMML, AICC Files, G-8, 1929, pts 1 & 22, Appendix 14, Desh Sevika Sangh.

74. NMML, AICC Files, G-8/1929, pts 1 & 23, Appendix 9, A Synopsis of Sardar Vallabhbhai's Advice to the Merchants and the Sevikas on 24th June, 1931.

75. NMML, AICC Files, G-8/1929, pts 1 & 2, Report of the Desh Sevika Sangh, 1931–1934, and Report of the Gandhi Seva Sena.

76. Interview with Latika Ghosh, Calcutta, Feb 29, 1976. Latika Ghosh was the daughter of Manmohan Ghosh and niece of Sri Aurobindo. She took the name Bose when she married in 1924. When the marriage was annulled in 1935, she resumed using the name Ghosh.

77. Ibid.

78. Latika Bose, "Mahila Rashtriya Sangha," *Banglar Katha* (Ashwin 11, 1335) [1928], np.; Latika Bose, *Banglar Katha* (Jaistha 22, 1335) [1928], p. 7.

79. Tanika Sarkar argued that women in India rarely made independent decisions to become politically involved but more frequently acted as "a sum and product of diverse relationships within the family and kinship nexus." Tanika Sarkar, "Politics and Women in Bengal—the Conditions and Meaning of Participation," *The Indian Economic and Social History Review*, 21: 1 (Jan-Mar, 1984), p. 91.

80. Bose, *Banglar Katha* (Ashwin 11, 1335).

81. Interview with Latika Ghosh, Calcutta. Feb 29, 1976 and Mar 10, 1976.

82. Ibid.

83. "Rally of Lady Volunteers," *Forward* (Dec 20, 1928), p. 7.

84. "All India Social Conference," *Forward* (Dec 20, 1928), p. 8; Interview with Renuka Ray, Calcutta, Apr 22, 1980.

85. Barbara Southard, "Bengal Women's Education League: Pressure Group and Professional Association," Modern *Asian Studies*, 18:1 (1984), pp. 55–88, 88.

86. Interview with Santi Das Kabir, New Delhi. Mar 25, 1976.

87. Ibid.

88. Ibid.

89. "Lively Scene in Burrabazar," *Amrita Bazaar Patrika [ABP]* (Jul 24, 1930), p. 3.

90. "Lady Satyagrahis Pass Night in the Street," ABP (Jul 26, 1930), p. 5.

91. See Geraldine Forbes, "Goddesses or Rebels? The Women Revolutionaries of Bengal," *The Oracle*, 2: 2 (Apr, 1980), pp. 1–12.

92. "Future of Indian Womanhood," *ABP* (Apr 29, 1931), p. 6.

93. "Srimati Saraladevi Chaudhurani's Speech at the Bengal Women's Congress," *Stri-Dharma*, 14 (Aug, 1931), pp. 508–10; "Women's Congress," *ABP* (May 2, 1931), p. 7.

94. Ibid.

95. Ibid.

96. Ibid.

97. "Bengal Women's Conference," *The Hindu* (May 3, 1931), p. 3; "Women's Congress," *ABP* (May 3, 1931), p. 7.

98. Tanika Sarkar's "Politics and Women in Bengal," which comments on women's involvement in Bankura, Midnapur, Comilla, and Noakali, and Jogesh C. Bagal's "Women in India's Freedom Movement," *The Modern Review*, 94 (Jan–Jun, 1953), pp. 467–80 and (Jul, 1953), pp. 53–61, are extremely useful for understanding Bengal. Studies now in progress will greatly add to historical literature on women's political activities.

99. *Fighters for Freedom*, vols 1 & 2 (Lucknow: Information Service, U.P., 1963, 1964).

100. Interview with Kamala Adhikari, South Canara Dist., May 27, 1976, trans. M. Ashton and L. Bhat.

101. Interview with Ambabai, Udipi, May 24, 1976, trans. Ashton and Bhat.

102. Gail Pearson, "Nationalism, Universalization and the Extended Female Space," in *The Extended Family: Women and Political Participation in India and Pakistan*, ed. Gail Minault (Delhi: Chanakya Publications, 1981), pp. 176–77.

103. From Table 8, "Convictions for Civil Disobedience, 1932–1933," in Judith Brown, *Gandhi and Civil Disobedience: the Mahatma in Indian Politics, 1928–1934* (Cambridge: Cambridge University Press, 1977), pp. 284–86.

CHAPTER 3: "WOMEN OF CHARACTER, GRIT, AND COURAGE"

1. It was because of Vina Mazumdar that I first wrote on the franchise issue in India. I met Vina in 1975, International Women's Year, and got to know her better in the winter of 1976. Vina welcomed me to her office and on numerous afternoons we talked about history and women's issues. What I recall most clearly are her questions about women's lives and the sources historians use. Fresh from her experiences as a member of the committee that wrote *Toward Equality,* an experience she has called " eye opening," she was skeptical about conventional accounts of women's history. It was due to her urging that I wrote "Votes for Women: The Demand for Women's Franchise in India, 1917–1937," for her edited book, *Symbols of Power: Studies on the Political Status of Women in India,* (Bombay: Allied, 1979). I revisited this topic, partly in response to the debates about reservations, and partly in response to Manju Parikh's invitation to join her, Usha Thakkar, and Mary Katzenstein on a panel, "Breaking Through the Barrier to Representation," at the Annual Meeting of the Association of Asian Studies, Chicago, 2001. I dedicate this paper to Vina who has been and will continue to be a person who asks hard questions, encourages me to dig deep for answers, and leads the way in thinking creatively about women's condition. She is a model, an inspiration, and a guiding light.
2. Mary E. John, "Alternate Modernities? Reservations and the Women's Movement in 20th Century India," *Economic and Political Weekly* [*EPW*], Oct 28, 2000, p. 3822.
3. Vijay Agnew, *Elite Women in Indian Politics* (New Delhi: Vikas, 1979); Jana Everett, *Women and Social Change in India* (New Delhi: Heritage, 1981); Janaki Nair, *Women and Law in Colonial India: A Social History* (New Delhi: Kali for Women, 1981).
4. Judith E. Walsh, "What Women Learned When Men Gave them Advice: Rewriting Patriarchy in Late-Nineteenth-Century Bengal," *Journal of Asian Studies,* 56: 3 (Aug, 1997), pp. 641–77.
5. "Ladies Deputation," *Indian Social Reformer,* 28 (Nov 11, 1917), p. 121.
6. *Report of the Special Section of the Indian National Congress, Bombay* (Aug 19–31 and Sep 1, 1918), (Bombay, 1918), pp. 109–10.

7. Fawcett Library [FL] *Fawcett Papers [FP]*: Letter from Dorothy Jinarajadasa to Dear Madam, Women's Indian Association, Nov 14, 1918, Box #70, and Letter to Chairman of the Franchise Committee, Nov 20, 1918, from 43 branches and 1400 members of the WIA, Box #90.

8. Great Britain [GB], *Parliamentary Papers [PP]*, 1919 [Cmd 203], Joint Select Committee on Government of India Bill, v. II, Minutes of Evidence, p. 75.

9. "Franchise for Indian Women," *Modern Review*, 26 (1919), p. 549.

10. The number of males enfranchised was small, the number of women voters infinitesimal. For example, male voters in Madras were slightly less than 12 percent of the adult male population while women voters were only 1 percent of adult females. Male voters were 5–13 percent of the adult male population in different provinces while women were 0.2—1 percent of the adult female population. Indian Statutory Commission, *Report of the Indian Statutory Commission [RISC]*, Volume I–Survey. May, 1930. [Cmd 3568]. (London, His Majesty's Stationery Office, 1930), p. 199.

11. Gail Pearson, "Reserved Seats—women and the vote in Bombay," *Indian Economic and Social History Review*, 20: 1 (Mar, 1983), p. 53.

12. Muthulakshmi used both Reddi and Reddy in signing her name. I have used Reddi in the text, and Reddy or Reddi in the footnotes depending on the document. Dr. (Mrs.) S. Muthulakshmi Reddy, *My Experiences As a Legislator*, (Madras: Current Thought Press, 1930). Her papers, including her views on franchise and her speeches, are in the Nehru Memorial Museum and Library.

13. Reddy, *My Experiences*, p. 4

14. "Women and the Vote," *Young India* (Nov 24, 1920), p. 2.

15. M.K. Gandhi, "Untouchability, Women and Swaraj," *Indian Social Reformer*, 37 (Mar 26, 1927), p. 465; Gandhi, "Speech at Women's Meeting," Coimbatore, Oct 16, 1927, *Collected Works of Mahatma Gandhi*, 25, (1969), p. 148.

16. Nair, p. 126

17. *RISC*, v. I and v. III, References to memorandum received from the Women's Medical Service and a Ladies Deputation led by the Maharani of Mandi.

18. *RISC*, III, pp. 93–94.

19. Ibid, pp. 78–79.
20. Ibid.
21. *RISC*, I, p. 53
22. Mrs. P. [Radhabai] Subbarayan, *The Political Status of Women Under the New Constitution* (Madras, np, nd), pp. 2–3; GB, *PP* 1930–1931, Indian Round Table Conference, November 12, 1930–January 19, 1931, [Cmd 3772], 47, p. 12.
23. "Reservations of Seats for Women," *The Hindu* (Nov 17, 1931), p. 5.
24. Pamphlet, no names or date, authored by M. Reddi, Correspondence Regarding Franchise, All India Women's Conference [AIWC] File #14, 1931.
25. The positions of women like Shah Nawaz changed with time and I have not done justice to either these changes or their complexity. For an excellent discussion of this topic see Jana Everett, " 'All the Women Were Hindu and All the Muslims Were Men,' State, Identity, Politics and Gender, 1917–1951," *EPW*, 36:23 (Jun 9, 2001), pp. 2071–80.
26. FL, *Rathbone Papers* [*RP*]: Letters from Mrs. P.N. Sirur to R. Subbarayan, Apr 22, 1931, R. Subbarayan to E. Rathbone, May 1, 1931, Folder #5; Letters from E. Rathbone to M. Reddi, Mar 12, 1931, M. Reddi to E. Rathbone, Mar 9, 1931, E. Rathbone to M. Reddi, May 1, 1931, M. Reddi to E. Rathbone, May 6, 1931, Folder #1.
27. These documents are not in the official report but with the Q papers. The Q papers are the uncatalogued and unpublished raw material collected by the committee. Dr. Richard Bingle allowed me to read through these boxes in Oriental and India Office Collection [OIOC].
28. OIOC, Indian Franchise Committee, 1932, Q/IFC/21–Bengal-Evidence File, E-Ben–132.
29. For example, Mrs. Salita Mukherji, representing the "Women of Bengal," recommended increasing the number of women voting through a literacy qualification and a lower property tax requirement, and allowing groups of 20 women, disenfranchised through other qualifications, one vote. Taken together, she argued these three schemes would enfranchise about 30% of the female population. Memo submitted by Mrs. Salita Mukherji, Sealdah House and

Memo on the Franchise Indian Franchise Committee, OIOC, 1932, Q/IFC/2,1-Bengal Evidence File, E–Ben–337 and E–Ben–460.

30. Ibid.
31. Everett, *Women and Social Change*, p. 122.
32. Everett, "All the Women," p. 2073.
33. Sushama Sen, *Memoirs of an Octogenarian* (Simla: Anjali, 1971), pp. 356–57.
34. *Stri Dharma,* 16 (Sep, 1933): p. 549; FC, *FP,* "Memorandum II on the Status of Women in the Proposed New Constitution of India," addressed to the members of the Joint Select Committee, June 1933, Pamphlet, Suffrage; GB, *PP,* 1932–1933, 8, (v.IIc), Minutes of Evidence given before the Joint Select Committee in the Indian Constitutional Reform, 1934, [House of Lords 79 (IIc)] [House of Commons 112 (IIc)], pp. 1617–22.
35. Renuka Ray, "Legal Disabilities of Indian Women," reprint from *Modern Review* (Nov, 1934); "Women's Movement in India," *Manchester Guardian* (Aug 15, 1935), AIWC Files #84.
36. Everett, *Women and Social Change*, p. 138.
37. WIA Report, 1936–1938, p. 27; "Women's Franchise in the New Constitution," *Indian Social Reformer,* 47, (Apr 24, 1937), p. 529; Manmohan Kaur in *The Role of Women in the Freedom Movement (1857–1947)* (New Delhi: Sterling 1968), pp. 204–5.
38. Appendix, Extracts from *Towards Equality*, "the Question of Reservation of Seats for Women in Legislative Bodies," Mazumdar, *Symbols of Power*, pp. 359–60.
39. John, p. 3828.
40. "Gandhiji on Women Legislators," *Indian Ladies Magazine* (Nov, 1931), p. 201.
41. John, p. 3828.
42. FC, *RP,* Folder #1, M. Reddi to E. Rathbone, Mar 31, 1933.

CHAPTER 4: MANAGING MIDWIFERY IN INDIA

1. Research for this paper was carried out in India and Great Britain with grants from the American Institute of Indian Studies, State University of New York Research Fund, and the National Endowment of the Humanities. My first thanks must go to Dagmar

Engels who encouraged me to write the paper and who has very kindly shared with me her insights and microfilm from the West Bengal State Archives. I am also indebted to Bill Freund and Sidney Greenblatt for their comments and suggestions regarding revision of the original paper. The opportunity provided by the German Historical Institute, London, to present this paper and listen to those of my colleagues at the Berlin Conference was invaluable.

2. *All India Women's Conference* [AIWC] *Report* (Calcutta, 1934), p. 150.

3. Vera Anstey, *The Economic Development of India* (London and New York: Longmans, Green, 1952) 1st Edn., 1929, Appendix A, pp. 489–91; also cited in Roger Jeffery, Patricia Jeffery and Andrew Lyon, "Only cord-cutters? Midwifery and childbirth in rural north India," *Social Action,* xxvii (1984), p. 1.

4. David Arnold, "Public health and public power: medicine and hegemony in colonial India," in *Contesting Colonial Hegemony: State and Society in Africa and India,* eds. Dagmar Engels and Shula Marks (London: German Historical Institute, London, British Academic Press, 1994), pp. 152–72.

5. Dwarka Nath Kakar, *Folk and Modern Medicine (A North Indian Case Study)* (Delhi: New Asian Publishers, 1977), p. 7.

6. Dr. P. Kutumbiah, *Ancient Indian Medicine* (Bombay: Orient Longman, 1962), pp. 177–94.

7. Dr. Julius Jolly, *Indian Medicine,* trans. from German by C.G. Kashikar (New Delhi: Munshiram Manoharlal, 1994), 1st Edn. 1951, p. 69.

8. Charles Leslie, "The modernization of Asian medical systems," in *Rethinking Modernization: Anthropological Perspectives,* ed. John J. Poggie and Robert. N. Lynch, (Westport, Conn.: Greenwood Press, 1971), pp. 69–108, esp. 89–90.

9. The *dhais* quoted in Jeffery, Jeffery and Lyon seemed to agree with these texts. These *dhais* had not read the texts but generally attributed difficulties in childbirth to a malformed fetus or failure to properly follow mandated ritual.

10. Jolly, Ch. 4; Kutumbiah, Ch. 9.

11. J. Fryer, MD, *A New Account of East India and Persia in Eight Letters* (London, 1698), p. 198.

12. Jean Donnison, *Midwives and Medical Men* (London: Heinemann Educational, 1977); Sir William Moore, *A Manual of Family Medicine*

and Hygiene for India, 7th Edn. (London: J. & A. Churchill, 1903); F.R. Hogg, *Practical Remarks Chiefly Concerning the Health and Ailments of European Families in India* (Benares, 1877).

13. B. Gupta, "Indigenous medicine in 19th and 20th-century Bengal," in *Asian Medical Systems: A Comparative Study,* ed. Charles Leslie (Berkeley, University of California Press, 1976), pp. 368–78, 370.

14. Ibid.

15. Roger Jeffery, *The Politics of Health in India* (Berkeley: University of California Press, 1988), p. 19.

16. James Mill, *The History of British India* (London: Baldwin, Cradock, and Joy, 1817) (Reprint New York, 1968), p. 303.

17. Kenneth Ballhatchet, *Race, Sex and Class Under the Raj* (London: Weidenfeld and Nicolson, 1980), pp. 10–39.

18. Jeffery, *The Politics of Health,* p. 20.

19. Lal Behari Day, *Bengal Peasant Life* (Calcutta: Editions Indian, 1970), 1st Edn. 1874, p. 21.

20. Dagmar Engels, "The changing role of women in Bengal, *c* 1890– *c* 1930, with special reference to British and Bengali discourse on gender," Ph.D. Dissertation (University of London, 1987), pp. 105–9. Published as Dagmar Engels, *Beyond Purdah? Women in Bengal, 1890–1939* (Delhi: Oxford University Press, 1996).

21. Meredith Borthwick, *The Changing Role of Women in Bengal, 1849–1905* (Princeton: Princeton University Press, 1984), pp. 156–64.

22. Ibid, pp. 154–55.

23. Ibid, pp. 159–60.

24. Geraldine Forbes, "In search of the 'pure heathen': missionary women in 19th-century India," *Economic and Political Weekly [EPW]* 21:17 (Apr 26, 1986), ws2-ws8.

25. Margaret Ida Balfour and Ruth Young, *The Work of Medical Women in India* (Oxford: Oxford University Press, 1929), pp. 13–14; Jeffery, *the Politics of Health,* pp. 89–91.

26. Balfour, *The Work of Medical Women,* pp. 15–18.

27. Jeffery, *The Politics of Health,* pp. 89–91.

28. Alice Wilkinson, *A Brief History of Nurses in India and Pakistan* (Delhi: Trained Nurses Association of India, 1958), p. 49; Marchioness of Dufferin and Ava, *Our Viceregal Life in India: Selections from My Journal, 1884–1888,* ii (London, 1889), p. 162.

29. *The Fifth Annual Report of the National Association for Supplying Medical Aid to the Women of India, For the Year 1889* (Calcutta: Superintendent of Government Printing, 1890), p. 20.

30. Ibid., pp. 48–49, 91.

31. Balfour, *The Work of Medical Women*, p. 38.

32. Mary Frances Billington, *Women in India* (London: Chapman & Hall, 1895)

33. *The Fifth Annual Report*, p. 99.

34. Malavika Karlekar, "Kadambini and the Bhadralok: early debates over women's education in Bengal," *EPW*, 21:17 (Apr 26, 1986), ws25–ws31.

35. Padmini Sengupta, *The Story of Women in India* (New Delhi: Indian Book Company, 1974), p. 160.

36. Mrs. Caroline Healy Dall, *The Life of Dr. Anandabai Joshee: A Kinswoman of the Pundhia Ramabai* (Boston: Roberts Brothers, 1988), pp. 88–90. Note: Anandabai is also spelled Anandibai and Joshee as Joshi.

37. "Dr. Rukhmabai; a pioneer medical woman of India," *World Medical Journal*, 2 (1964), pp. 35–6. A more recent study of Rukhmabai's case was published in 1998. See Sudhir Chandra, *Enslaved Daughters: Colonialism, Law and Women's Rights* (Delhi: Oxford University Press, 1998).

38. H. Lazarus, *Autobiography of Hilda May Lazarus* (Vizagapatnam, nd.), pp. 1–5; Hilda Lazarus, Interview, Vizagapatnam, Jan 30, 1976.

39. Balfour, *The Work of Medical Women*, p. 126.

40. Engels, "The changing role," Ch. 6; Anstey, *Economic Development*, p. 70.

41. Great Britain, *Parliamentary Papers*, Report of the Royal Commission on Labour in India, 1930–31, xi, [Cmd 3883], pp. 261–63.

42. Ibid.

43. Janet Harvey. Kelman, *Labour in India: A Study of the Conditions of Indian Women in Modern Industry* (London and New York: Selly Oak Colleges Publications, 1923), pp. 219–23.

44. *Royal Commission on Labour*, pp. 411–12.

45. Engels, "The changing role," pp. 209–12.

46. *Special Report on the Working of Act 1 of 1882 in the Province of Assam During the Years 1886–1889*, part 4 (Calcutta, 1890), p. 707.

47. Balfour, *The Work of Medical Women*, p. 145.

48. Anstey, *Economic Development*, pp. 88–89.

49. Lady Cowasji Jehangir, "Maternal welfare work in Bombay," *The Asiatic Review*, 33 (Oct, 1937), pp. 759–67.

50. Bombay Presidency Women's Council [BPWC] 6th Annual Report (1924–5), p. 8.

51. BPWC, 11th Annual Report (1928–9), p. 28.

52. BPWC, 6th Annual Report, pp. 17–18.

53. BPWC, 11th Annual Report.

54. National Council of Women in India, 4th Biennial Report (1932–4), Resolution 13.

55. AIWC, 5th Annual Report (Lahore, 1931), p. 63.

56. AIWC, 6th Annual Report (Madras, 1932), p. 81.

57. AIWC: 6th Annual Report, p. 81; 7th Annual Report (Lucknow, 1933), p. 90; 8th Annual Report (Calcutta, 1934), p. 131; 9th Annual Report (Karachi, 1935), p. 85.

58. AIWC: 8th Annual Report, p. 150.

59. Anstey, *Economic Development*, p. 69.

60. The earliest act was passed in 1926 in Madras, then similar acts were passed in the Punjab (1932), Bengal and UP (1934), Bombay and Bihar and Orissa (1935), and Central Provinces (1936). See Wilkinson, *A Brief History of Nurses in India*, pp. 58, 88–9; *Bombay Legislative Council Debates Official Reports* [BLCD], February-March 1935 Session (Bombay, 1935), pp. 1641–43, 1677–78.

61. *BLCD*, p. 1643.

62. *Sixth Annual Report of the National Association for Supplying Medical Aid to the Women of India*, For the Year 1890, (Calcutta, Superintendent of Government Printing, 1891), p. 222.

63. *Fourth Annual Report of Madras Branch of the Countess of Dufferin's Fund*, (Madras, 1889), p. 7.

64. Ibid.

65. Balfour, *The Work of Medical Women*, p. 20.

66. Shudha Mazumdar, *Memoirs of an Indian Women*, ed. Geraldine Forbes (New York: M.E. Sharpe, 1989), pp. 112–13; 162–63.

67. Interview with Shudha Mazumdar, Calcutta, Jun, 1972.

68. Mazumdar, *Memoirs*, p. 175.

69. David Arnold, "Medical priorities and practice in 19th-century British India," *South Asia Research*, 5 (1985), pp. 167–83: 179.

CHAPTER 5: EDUCATION TO EARN

1. "First Annual Meeting of the National Association for Supplying Medical Aid to the Women of India, Town Hall, Calcutta, 27 January 1885," included in the *First Annual Report of the National Association for Supplying Medical Aid to the Women of India*, January, 1886 (Calcutta, 1886), pp. 79–80.

2. Sarala Ray, "Notes on Female Education," *Sarala Ray Centenary Volume* (Calcutta: Sarala Ray Centenary Committee, 1961), pp. 10–11.

3. Y.B. Mathur, *Women's Education in India (1813—1966)*. (Bombay: Asia Publishing House, 1973), pp. 40–42.

4. Shefali Chandra, "Between the Burkha and the Ballroom. The English educated woman in the nineteenth century," Paper presented at the 31st Annual Conference on South Asia. University of Wisconsin, Madison (2002).

5. Ibid.

6. Partha Chatterjee, *The Nation and Its Fragments: Colonial and Postcolonial Histories* (Princeton: Princeton University Press, 1993).

7. Judith E. Walsh, "What Women Learned When Men Gave them Advice: Rewriting Patriarchy in Late-Nineteenth-Century Bengal," *Journal of Asian Studies*, 56: 3, (Aug, 1997), pp. 641–77.

8. David Arnold, *Imperial Medicine and Indigenous Societies* (Delhi: Oxford University Press, 1989); David Arnold, *Colonizing the Body* (Berkeley: University of California Press, 1993); Mark Harrison, *Public Health in British India* (Cambridge: Cambridge University Press, 1994).

9. See Philippa Levine, "Venereal Disease, Prostitution and the Politics of Empire: The Case of British India," *Journal of the History of Sexuality*, 4: 4 (1994), pp. 579–602. Professor Levine's exhaustive study of the Contagions Diseases [CD] Acts in the colonies was published as *Prostitution, Race and Politics: Policing Venereal Disease in the British Empire* (New York: Routledge, 2003).

10. Oriental and India Office Collection [OIOC], v/24/2292, Medical, 1877, Lock Hospitals, Resolution (Jul 17, 1878) Darjeeling.

11. Geraldine Forbes, "In Search of the Pure Heathen: Missionary Women in Nineteenth Century India," *Economic and Political Weekly*, 21:17 (Apr 26, 1986), ws2-ws8.

12. Rosemary Fitzgerald, "A 'Peculiar and Exceptional Measure': The

Call for Women Medical Missionaries for India in the Later
Nineteenth Century," *Missionary Encounters: Sources and Issues*, eds.
R. Bickers and R. Seton, (London: Curzon Press, 1996), pp. 174–
97; Rosemary Fitzgerald, "'Rescue and Redemption'–The Rise
of Female Medical Missions in Colonial India During the Late
Nineteenth and Early Twentieth Centuries," *Nursing History and The
Politics of Welfare*, eds. A.M. Rafferty, J. Robinson, and R. Elkan
(London: Routledge, 1996), pp. 64–79.

13. "Medical Women for India," *Proceedings of the Northwest Provinces
and Oudh Branch of the British Medical Association*, 2:2 (Apr, 1883),
pp. 130–31.

14. Supriya Guha, "A History of the Medicalisation of Childbirth in
Bengal in the Late Nineteenth and Early Twentieth Centuries,"
Ph.D. Dissertation (University of Calcutta, 1996), p. 109.

15. Meredith Borthwick, *The Changing Role of Women in Bengal, 1849–
1905* (Princeton: Princeton University Press, 1984), pp. 156–57.

16. Madras Political Proceedings, Letter No. 42, from Edward Balfour,
Government Agent to the Nawab of Carnatic, to Montgomery, Bart.,
Chief Secretary to the Government, Aug 8, 1853 (courtesy Sylvia
Vatuk).

17. Margaret I. Balfour and Ruth Young, *The Work of Medical Women in
India* (Oxford: Oxford University Press, 1929), p. 13.

18. Government of India Archives, Home, Medical, June 1886, "What
has been done in the Punjab for the Medical Training and Treatment
of Women," Report of J. Fairweather, Officiating Inspector-General
of Civil Hospitals, Punjab, Aug 19, 1885 (courtesy Rosemary
Fitzgerald).

19. Borthwick, p. 159

20. The numbers are as follows: 1892: 7 native *dhais* and 13 pupil-nurses;
1893: 10 native *dhais* and 13 pupil-nurses; 1894: 9 native *dhais* and 15
pupil-nurses; 1895: 17 native *dhais* and 16 pupil-nurses; 1896: 8 native
dhais and 19 pupil-nurses; 1898: 15 native *dhais* and 14 pupil-nurses;
1899: 7 native *dhais* and 17 pupil-nurses. *General Report of Public
Instruction in Bengal [GRPIB], 1891–92* (Calcutta: Bengal Secretariat
Press, 1892), p. 78; *GRPIB, 1892–93* (1893), p. 97; *GRPIB, 1893–94*
(1894), p. 97; *GRPIB, 1894–95* (1895); *GRPIB, 1895–96* (1896), p.
91; *GRPIB, 1897–98* (1898), p. 88; *GRPIB, 1898–99* (1899), p. 107.

21. See Geraldine Forbes, "Managing Midwifery in India," in this volume.

22. *The Countess of Dufferin's Fund—the Sixth Annual Report of the National Association for Supplying Female Medical Aid to the Women of India, Burma Branch, for the Year 1892* (Calcutta: Office of the Superintendent of Government Printing, 1893), pp. 13–14.

23. Barbara Ramusack is currently working on maternal and child welfare in British India and the native states. She has presented a number of papers on this topic including "Motherhood and Medical Intervention: Women's Bodies and Professionalism in India After World War I," (Madison, 1996), "Maternal and Infant Health Initiatives: Madras and Mysore, 1870–1930," (Oxford, 1996), and "Issues of Equity: Maternal Medical Facilities in Rural Mysore, 1880–1920," (Madison, 1997).

24. Guha, pp. 122–24.

25. *Report of the Bengal Branch of the Countess of Dufferin's Fund 30 March 1902*, nd. p. 8. Lieut. Col. D. G. Crawford, in the *Hughli Medical Gazetteer*, wrote that most *dhais* were Haris or Mochis by caste. He said that the *dhai* received 4 annas for the delivery of a male child and 2 annas for a female child from the lower classes, as well as a meal of rice and vegetables, and that the higher classes gave more but never more than Rs 3, cloth, and brass vessels. In towns, people paid *dhais* Rs 5–8 when the first child was born and Rs 1–5 for a male child and 8 annas–Rs 2 for a female. (Calcutta, Bengal Secretariat Press, 1902), p. 394.

26. Philippa Levine has informed me that the *dhais* employed to check prostitutes under the CD Acts were not allowed speculums although doctors who performed the inspections used them.

27. *Seventeenth Annual Report of the Bengal Branch of the National Association for Supplying Medical Aid to the Women of India* (1902), pp. 9–16.

28. *Twenty-fourth Annual Report of the Bengal Branch of the Countess of Dufferin Fund—for the year ending 30 November 1909* (Calcutta, 1910), p. 6.

29. *Twenty-Sixth Annual Report of the National Association for Supplying Medical Aid to the Women of India for the Year 1910*, nd, pp. 64–65.

30. Barbara Ramusack, in unpublished papers (see fn 17) makes the case that governments in the South were far more interested in training midwives than seems to have been the case in Bengal.

31. For example, see "Sutika Griho," [Room for the birth of the baby], an article written by a woman urging women to become aware of "modern" birthing practices, published in *Antpur*, a women's magazine, (Kartik, 1902) (5th year) pp. 134–38.

32. Dagmar Engels, *Beyond Purdah? Women in Bengal 1890–1939* (Delhi: Oxford University Press, 1996), pp. 123–57.

33. OIOC, Cornelia Sorabji Papers, Note on the Possibilities Appertaining to a Social Service Institute.

34. *The Bengalee* (Jan 3, 189), p. 12.

35. "Dr. Sundarimohan Das (1857–1950)," *Dictionary of National Biography*, ed. S.P. Sen, I, (Calcutta: Calcutta Historical Institute, 1972), p. 363.

36. E. M. Tonge, *Fanny Jane Butler: Pioneer Medical Missionary* (London, Church of England Missionary Society, nd), J. L. M., "Fanny Jane Butler, L.K.Q.C.P.I., and L.M.," *Medical Missions at Home and Abroad*, 3 (January, 1890), pp. 52–59.

37. Antoinette Burton, "Contesting the Zenana: The Mission to Make 'Lady Doctors for India,' 1874–1885," *Journal of British Studies*, 35 (Jul, 1996), pp. 368–97, 369.

38. O.P. Jaggi, *History of Science, Technology and Medicine in India*, v. 13 *Western Medicine in India: Medical Education and Research*, (Delhi and Lucknow, Atma Ram and Sons, 1979), p. 93. Graduating with Scharlieb in 1878 were Miss D. White, Miss D. Mitchell, and Miss B. Beate.

39. Chandrika Paul, "The Uneasy Alliance: The Work of British and Bengali Women Medical Professionals in Bengal: 1870–1935," Dissertation, University of Cincinnati (1977), pp. 65–66.

40. Paul, pp. 69–76.

41. *Commemorative Volume, On the Occasion of Golden Jubilee Reunion and Terjubilee Year of Medical College, Calcutta* (Calcutta: np, 1984), p. 66

42. *The Life of Anandabai Joshee (sic)*, by Mrs. Caroline Healey Dall (Boston: Roberts Brothers, 1888), pp. 85–86. "Dr. Anandibai Joshee," *Indian Ladies Magazine*, 7 (January, 1934), pp. 315–16. Note: Anandabai is also spelled Anandibai and Joshi as Joshee.

43. Mridula Ramanna, "Indian Practitioners of Western Medicine: Grant Medical College, 1845–1885," *Radical Journal of Health* (New Series), (Bombay), 1:2 (1995), pp. 116–35, 120.

44. Only three of these women were "Bengali," the others were European, Eurasian, Armenian, Portuguese, and Jewish women domiciled in Bengal.

45. "The Lady Dufferin Fund and the Indian Lady Doctor," *The Bengalee* (Feb 7, 1891), p. 65.
46. "The Zenana Hospital and Suggestions to the Committee," *The Bengalee* (Mar 7, 1891), p. 112.
47. "The Bangabasi Case," *Indian Messenger* (Jul 12, 1891), p. 346
48. *Tenth Annual Report*, p. 156.
49. Interview with Parul Bose, Calcutta (Mar 13, 1893).
50. In 1883 Brigade Surgeon Hilson proposed a class for women hospital assistants at Agra and by 1885, there were 21 candidates enrolled. Jaggi, p. 103.
51. Published in *Bharat Mihir* (Jul, 1876), located in a file in the National Library, Calcutta, quoted by Chandrika Paul, "The Uneasy Alliance: The Work of British and Bengali Women Medical Professionals in Bengal: 1870–1935."
52. West Bengal State Archives [WBSA]. To Secretary of Government of Bengal, From: Surgeon-Major A. Crombie, Superintendent, Medical School, Dacca, July, 1887 [File 21-26]. Proceedings of the Lieutenant Governor of Bengal, General Dept., Education.
53. WBSA. To: Secretary of Government of Bengal, from: Surgeon-Major C.J.W. Meadows, officiating Civil Surgeon, Patna, General Dept. Aug 11, 1887, Ibid.
54. WBSA. To: Secretary of Government of Bengal, from: Sir A.W. Croft, Director of Public Instruction, Bengal, "Female Medical Education," Apr 29, 1887. No. 2751, Calcutta, Ibid.
55. *The Indian Messenger* (Aug 2, 1891), p. 369.
56. *General Report on Public Instruction in Bengal, 1892–1893* (Calcutta: Bengal Secretariat Press, 1893), p. 72.
57. *General Report on Public Instruction in Bengal, 1890–1891* (Calcutta: Bengal Secretariat Press, 1891), p. 68.
58. These issues were discussed prior to building Lady Hardinge Medical College for Women in Delhi. Lady Hardinge opened in 1916.
59. Quoted in Jogesh C. Bagal, "History of the Bethune School and College (1849–1949)," ed. Kalidas Nag, *Bethune School and College Centenary Volume, 1849–1949* (Calcutta: Bethune School and College Centenary Volume Subcommittee, nd), p. 43.
60. Maneesha Lal, "The Politics of Gender and Medicine in Colonial India: The Countess of Dufferin's Fund, 1885–1888," *Bulletin of the History of Medicine*, 68 (1994), p. 65.

61. *General Report of Public Instruction in Bengal, 1894–95* (Calcutta: Bengal Secretariat Press, 1895), p. 83.

CHAPTER 6: MEDICINE FOR WOMEN

1. I used the same spelling of names as used in official records even when these deviate from conventional use.
2. I use "lady doctor" throughout this essay because these women were referred to by this term.
3. *Tenth Annual Report of the National Association for Supplying Female Medical Aid to the Women of India for the Year 1894* (Calcutta: Office of the Superintendent of Government Printing, India, 1865), p. 161.
4. *Report of the Bengal Branch of the Countess of Dufferin's Fund for the Year Ending 30 November 1903* (nd.), p. 1.
5. *Report of the Bengal Branch of the Countess of Dufferin's Fund for the Year Ending 30 November 1896* (nd.), p. 8.
6. For example, see: Margaret I. Balfour and Ruth Young, *The Work of Medical Women in India* (Oxford: Oxford University Press, 1929); Roger Jeffrey, *The Politics of Health in India* (Berkeley: University of California Press, 1987); David Arnold, *Imperial Medicine and Indigenous Societies* (Delhi: Oxford University Press, 1989); David Arnold, *Colonizing the Body* (Berkeley: University of California Press, 1993), Poonam Bala, *Imperialism and Medicine in Bengal* (New Delhi: Sage Publications, 1991); Mark Harrison, *Public Health in British India* (Cambridge: Cambridge University Press, 1994); Malavika Karlekar, "Kadambini and the Bhadralok," *Economic and Political Weekly*, 21:19 (Apr 26, 1986); Maneesha Lal, "The Politics of Gender and Medicine in Colonial India: The Countess of Dufferin's Fund, 1885–1888," *Bulletin of the History of Medicine*, 68 (1994); Antoinette Burton, "Contesting the Zenana: the Mission to Make 'Lady Doctors for India,' 1874–1885," *Journal of British Studies*, 35:3 (Jul, 1996); Chandrika Paul, "Uncaging the Birds: the Entrance of Bengali Women into Medical Colleges 1870–1890," Paper presented at Mid-West Conference on Asian Affairs, Cleveland, Ohio (1993); Supriya Guha, "A History of the Medicalisation of Childbirth in Bengal in the Late Nineteenth and Early Twentieth Centuries," Ph.D. Dissertation, (University of Calcutta, 1996); and Mridula Ramana,

Western Medicine and Public Health in Colonial Bombay, 1845–1895 (Orient Longman Ltd., 2002).

7. West Bengal State Archive [WBSA], Home Department 1874, Medical, B Proceedings, April, Nos. 12–17, Subject: "Transfer of the Vernacular Classes from the Medical College to Sealdah."

8. From 1913 the degree awarded was LMP. In 1914 the State Medical Faculty took over the function of examining the students. In 1937 the government recommended the end of dual standards.

9. WBSA, Proceedings of the Lieutenant-Governor of Bengal, March 1879, General Dept., Education [Destroyed Files].

10. Dr. (Mrs.) Usha Chakraborty, *Condition of Bengali Women Around the 2nd Half of the 19th Century* (Calcutta: Usha Chakraborty, 1963), pp. 180–81.

11. Aparna Basu, "The Role of Women in the Indian Struggle for Freedom," *Indian Women: From Purdah to Modernity*, ed. B.R. Nanda (New Delhi: Vikas, 1976), p. 17.

12. The Sadharan Brahmo Samaj was formed in 1878 after a schism in the Brahmo Samaj. Sadharan Brahmos made efforts to improve the condition of women through education, later age of marriage, remarriage or training of widows, the introduction of western medicine, and the encouragement of social equality.

13. WBSA, Proceedings of the Lieutenant Governor of Bengal, General Department, Education, No. 2751, Calcutta [File 21–26], To: Secretary of Government of Bengal, from: Sir A.W. Croft, Director of Public Instruction, Bengal, "Female Medical Education, April 29, 1887".

14. Also spelled Swarnamayi and Surnomoyi.

15. To: Secretary of Government of Bengal, from Sir A.W. Croft.

16. WBSA, Proceedings of the Lieutenant Governor of Bengal, General Department, Education, No. 2751, To: Secretary of Government of Bengal, from: S.C. Mackenzie, Superintendent, Campbell Medical School; General Dept., Jul 15, 1887.

17. WBSA, Ibid, To: Secretary of Government of Bengal, from: Surgeon-Major A. Crombie, Superintendent, Medical School, Dacca, July, 1887.

18. WBSA, Ibid, To: Secretary of Government of Bengal, from: Surgeon-Major C.J.W. Meadows, Officiating Civil Surgeon, Patna, General Dept. Aug 11, 1887.

19. WBSA, Ibid, To: Secretary of Government of Bengal, from: Dr. R.L. Dutt, Officiating Civil Surgeon in Rungpore.

20. The exact number of students in this first class varies in different accounts. *The Bengalee* (Jul 7,1888), p. 313, carried an article saying 15 "Native Young Ladies" had been admitted into the program at Campbell. The article said many of them were Brahmins; only three had passed the middle school vernacular exam, the rest passed the special entrance exam. Ten of the students were admitted with scholarships, the others were admitted without fees. *The Fourth Annual Report of the National Association for Supplying Female Medical Aid to the Women of India, January 1889* (Calcutta: Office of Government Printing, 1889), p. 16, says 17 students were admitted to the first class in 1988 but six months later only 15 remained. However, *The National Association for Supplying Female Medical Aid*, 1885–1888, p. 40, a short book published to summarize the yearly reports, says thirteen pupils were admitted: eight Hindus, two Brahmos, two native Christians, and one East Indian. According to the *Sixth Annual Report of The National Association for Supplying Female Medical Aid to the Women of India, for the Year 1890* (Calcutta: Office of Government Printing, 1891), p. 131, there were only 11 students remaining in December of that year. This second year class included: Sreemati Hari Mati Dasi, Smt. Kiron Sashi Mukerjea, Smt. Kailas Basini Guha, Miss Sashi Mukhi Nath, Smt Jadumoni Debi, Mrs. S. M. Biswas, Smt. Hemangini Debi, Smt. Basanta Kumari Gupta, Miss Agnes Cecilia Bastien, Smt. Khiroda Sundari Roy, and Smt. Sarat Kumari Mitra. Except for Haimabati Sen, I have preserved the way their names are written in official documents.

21. *General Report of Public Instruction in Bengal, 1889– 90* (Calcutta: Bengal Secretariat Press, 1890), p. 69.

22. *Report of the Bengal Branch of the Countess of Dufferin Fund for the Year Ending 30 November 1904* (Calcutta: Bengal Secretariat Press, 1905), pp. 36–43.

23. *The memoirs of Dr. Haimabati Sen: from child widow to lady doctor*, translated by Tapan Raychaudhuri, edited by Geraldine Forbes and Tapan Raychaudhuri, introduced by Geraldine Forbes (New Delhi: Roli Books Ltd., 2002).

24. The list of the 1891 class (with ages): Smt. Kadambini Banerjea

29), Smt. Mokhoda Roy (23), Smt. Sarna Lata Mitra (17), Smt. Benoy Kumari Chuckerbutty (16), Mrs. Jaggat Tarini Banerjea (26), Miss Indu Mukhi Dey (18), Mrs. Annandamoyi Bhattacharjea (29), Smt. Shodosi Bala Ghose (18), Mussamut Idennessa (16), Smt. Kadambini Sen Gupta (17), Smt. Lukhi Bala Bose (23), Miss Lilawvati Ghosh (17), Smt. Hemabati Sen (26). *Seventh Annual Report of the National Association for Supplying Female Medical Aid to Women of India, 1891* (Calcutta: Office of Government Printing, 1892), p. 60. Their names are spelled as they occurred in the British records.

25. *Seventh Annual Report of the National Association, 1891,* p. 105.
26. *Centenary of Medical College Bengal, 1835–1934* (Calcutta, 1935).
27. *General Report of Public Instruction in Bengal, 1899–1900* (Calcutta: Bengal Secretariat Press, 1900), p. 109.
28. *Ninth Annual Report, 1893,* pp. 142–43.
29. *List of Qualified Medical Practitioners in Bengal 1930.* Compiled in the office of the Inspector General of Civil Hospitals, Bengal (Calcutta: Bengal Secretariat Press, 1903).
30. In 1994 I interviewed Mrs. Radha Rani Chatterjee, a retired English teacher from Chinsurah, who was then in her 70s. She said her father told her about Dr. Sen when she was a little girl. He admired Haimabati, called her a woman of "high culture," and related that she had to fight for her education. Mrs. Chatterjee commented that she, like Haimabati, had to fight for her education and was supported every step of the way by her father.
31. *The Seventeenth Annual Report of the Bengal Branch of the National Association for Supplying Medical Aid to the Women of India* (Calcutta: Bengal Secretariat Press, 1902), p. 14.
32. *Report of the Bengal Branch of the Countess of Dufferin's Fund. 30th November 1989.* (nd.) p. 5.
33. *Report of the Bengal Branch of the Countess of Dufferin's Fund. 30th November 1903.* (nd.) p. 1.
34. Rosemary Fitzgerald, "A 'Peculiar and Exceptional Measure': The Call for Women Medical Missionaries for India in the Later Nineteenth Century," *Missionary Encounters: Sources and Issues,* ed. R. Bickers and R. Seton (London: Curzon Press, 1996), pp. 174–97.
35. *Report of the Bengal Branch of the Countess of Dufferin's Fund for the Year Ending 30th November 1896* (nd.), p. 88.
36. *The Twenty-first Annual Report of the Bengal Branch of the National*

Association for Supplying Female Medical Aid to the Women of India, 1906 (Calcutta: Bengal Secretariat Press, 1907), p. 10.

37. *Seventeenth Annual Report*, pp. 11–14.

38. *Ninth Annual Report*, 1893, pp. 146–47.

39. *Twenty-third Annual Report of the National Association for Supplying Female Medical Aid to the Women of India, 1907* (Calcutta: Office of the Superintendent, 1908), pp. 10–12.

40. *Annual Returns of the Charitable Dispensaries under the Government of Bengal for the year 1899* (Calcutta: Bengal Secretariat Press, 1900), pp. 1–2.

41. *Triennial Report on the working of the Charitable Dispensaries under the Government of Bengal and the Calcutta Medical Institutions for the Years 1899, 1900, and 1901* (Calcutta: Bengal Secretariat Press, 1902), p. 25.

42. Peary Mohun Banerjee, Deputy Magistrate, Branch Dufferin, Hooghly, *Report of the Bengal Branch of the Countess of Dufferin Fund for the Year Ending 30th November 1897* (nd.), p. 77.

43. *Report of the Bengal Branch of the Countess of Dufferin Fund for the Year Ending 30th November 1901* (nd.), p. 4; *The Twenty-first Annual Report of the Bengal Branch*, p. 10.

44. *Seventeenth Annual Report*, p. 12.

45. *Tenth Annual Report*, p. 154.

46. Arnold, *Colonizing the Body*, p. 265.

47. *Annotated Returns of the Charitable Dispensaries in Bengal for the Year, 1893* by Surgeon General Robert Harvey (Calcutta: Bengal Secretariat Press, 1894), p. 3.

48. *Tenth Annual Report*, p. 151.

49. *Triennial Report on the working of the Charitable Dispensaries under the Government of Bengal for the Years 1893, 1894, and 1895* (Calcutta: Bengal Secretariat Press, 1896), p. xii. It is difficult to trace the number of operations Dr. Sen performed each year because the classification system changed. In the early 1890s operations were classified as major and minor but this classification was dropped by 1896 in some reports, obfuscated in others. The following list gives some idea of the procedures considered "operations:" extraction of lens, excision of upper and lower jaw, lithotomy, removal of scrotal tumor and elephantiasis of scrotum, delivery by forceps, embryotomy (craniotomy), amputations, removal of tumors, opening abscesses,

extraction of teeth, opening of gumboil, and removal of diseased lymphatic glands. *Annual Returns of the Charitable Dispensaries under the Government of Bengal for the year 1896* (Calcutta: Bengal Secretariat Press, 1897): p. xxxvii.

50. *Report of the Bengal Branch*, 1896, p. 88.
51. *Report of the Bengal Branch*, 1897, pp. 77–78.
52. *Report of the Bengal Branch of the Countess of Dufferin Fund for the Year Ending 30ᵗʰ November 1900* (nd.), p. 134.
53. *Report of the Bengal Branch, 1900*, p. 135.
54. *Report of the Bengal Branch*, 1900, p. 9.

CHAPTER 7: THE FIRST STEP IN WRITING WOMEN'S HISTORY

1. I refer to Shudha Mazumdar as "Shudha" and other Indian women in this paper by their given names. This conforms to Indian usage and is not considered rude or familiar.
2. Hasi Banerjee, *Sarojini Naidu: The Traditional Feminist* (Calcutta: K.P. Bagchi, 1998), p. 71; Sarojini Naidu, "Advice to City Fathers of Karachi," *Forward* (Aug 16, 1925), p. 15.
3. Mary Daly, *Gyn/Ecology: The Metaethics of Radical Feminism* (Boston: Beacon Press, 1990).
4. Katherine Mayo, *Mother India* (London: Jonathan Cape, 1927).
5. Mrinalini Sinha. Ed., *Mother India: Selections from the Controversial 1927 Text* (Ann Arbor, Michigan: The University of Michigan Press, 2000).
6. Shudha Mazumdar, *Memoirs of an Indian Woman*, ed. Geraldine Forbes (Armonk, N.Y.: M.E. Sharpe, 1989); Manmohini Zutshi Sahgal, *An Indian Freedom Fighter Recalls Her Life*, ed. Geraldine Forbes (Armonk, N.Y.: M.E. Sharpe, 1994); *The memoirs of Dr. Haimabati Sen: from child widow to lady doctor*, eds. Geraldine Forbes and Tapan Raychaudhuri, trans. Tapan Raychaudhuri (New Delhi: Roli Books Ltd. 2000); and Lakshmi Sahgal, *A Revolutionary Life: Memoirs of A Political Activist*, introduction by Geraldine Forbes (New Delhi: Kali for Women, 1989).
7. See, for example, Tanika Sarkar, *Words to Win: The Making of Amar Jiban: A Modern Autobiography* (New Delhi: Kali for Women, 1999); *Binodini Dasi: My Story and My Life As An Actress*, ed. and trans.

Rimli Bhattacharya (New Delhi: Kali for Women, 1998); Rosalind O'Hanlon, *A comparison between women and men : Tarabai Shinde and the critique of gender relations in colonial India* (Madras: Oxford University Press, 1994); Malavika Karlekar, *Writing Voices From Within* (Delhi: Oxford University Press, 1991); and Stree Shakti Sanghatana, "*We were making history …*" *Life stories of women in the Telangana People's Struggle* (New Delhi: Kali for Women, 1989).

8. See, for example, Roger Jeffrey, *The Politics of Health in India* (Berkeley: University of California Press, 1987); David Arnold, *Imperial Medicine and Indigenous Societies* (Delhi: Oxford University Press, 1989); David Arnold, *Colonizing the Body* (Berkeley: University of California Press, 1993); Poonam Bala, *Imperialism and Medicine in Bengal* (New Delhi: Sage Publications, 1991); Mark Harrison, *Public Health in British India*, (Cambridge: Cambridge University Press, 1994).

9. There does not seem to be a complete collection of the Dufferin Fund records in any library. Those I have used in the Oriental and India Office Library, the National Library in Kolkata, the National Archives in Delhi, and the Maharashtrian State Archives, are excellent sources for research on Indian women.

10. *Amhihi Ithihas Ghadawala: Urmila Pawar and the Making of History*, ed. Roshan G. Shahani, Publication No. 6. (Mumbai: SPARROW, 1998); *The World as My Laboratory-Shantoo Gurnani's Tryst With Science*, ed. Roshan G. Shahani, Publication No. 3. (Mumbai: SPARROW, 1998); *Pramila-Esther Victoria Abraham*, ed. Roshan G. Shahani, Publication No. 2. (Mumbai: SPARROW, 1998); *Jameela Nishat: A Poem Slumbers in My Heart*, ed. Roshan G. Shahani, Publication No. 11. (Mumbai: SPARROW, 1999). SPARROW has published 12 booklets, two books, and a number of booklets in translation.

11. Ralph W. Nicholas, "Listening to What People Tell You: The Cultural Study of Indian Society," unpublished paper (1974).

12. Krishnabai, Nimbkar. Interview by Hari Dev Sharma. Tape recording and Transcript. Oral History Project on Freedom Fighters. Nehru Memorial Museum and Library. Dec 10, 1984.

13. Krishnabai, Nimbkar. Pune. Interview, May 31, 1983.

14. Samuel Bourne, a British photographer, traveled extensively in India in the 1860s photographing landscapes and historical sites. He and Charles Shepherd, a noted printer, went into business in Calcutta as Bourne and Shepherd Studios and became famous for their

photographs of colonial India. When the studio burned in the 1980s thousands of glass plate negatives and photographs were destroyed.

15. In Dec, 2001, the Centre for Women's Development Studies held its first exhibit of women's photographs: "Re-Presenting Indian Women 1875–1947," at the India International Centre's Art Gallery. Dr. Malavika Karlekar was the exhibition curator and has been at the forefront of an effort to establish an archive of women's photographs. CWDS has arranged its photo archive in six categories: family, education, worlds beyond, the Freedom Struggle, independence, and creativity.

CHAPTER 8: REFLECTIONS ON SOUTH ASIAN WOMEN'S HISTORY

1. The Conference on Rhetoric and Reality: Gender and the Colonial Experience, sponsored by the Association of Commonwealth Universities, the University of London's School of Oriental and African Studies, and the International Federation for Research in Women's History, was held in Dhaka, Bangladesh, Dec 17–18, 2002. This conference, organized by the Bangladesh Chapter of the International Federation for Research in Women's History, conceived of and developed by Sonia Nishat Amin and Avril Powell, was Bangladesh's first conference on women's history.

2. For a comprehensive review see Barbara Ramusack, "Women in South Asia," in Barbara Ramusack and Sharon Sievers, *Women in Asia: Restoring Women to History* (Bloomington: Indiana University Press, 1999). Also see the bibliographic essay in Geraldine Forbes, *Women in Modern India* (Cambridge: Cambridge University Press, 1996), and Geraldine Forbes, "Women's Studies," *India's Worlds and U.S. Scholars: 1947–1997*, eds. Joseph W. Elder, Edward C. Dimock, and Ainslie T. Embree (Delhi: Manohar, 1998), pp. 569–89.

3. A good example is A.S. Altekar's *The Position of Women in Hindu Civilization* (Benares: Benares Hindu University, 1938; 2nd Edn., Delhi: Motilal Banarsidass, 1959, reprinted 1978, 1983).

4. Neera Desai, *Woman in Modern India* (Bombay: Vora and Co., 1957) 2nd Edn. 1977.

5. For example, Manmohan Kaur's *Role of Women in the Freedom*

Movement 1857–1947 (New Delhi: Sterling, 1968), celebrated women's political achievements. Autobiographies and biographies, featuring prominent women such as Sarojini Naidu, Muthulakshmi Reddy, and Vijayalakshmi Pandit appeared at this time.

6. *Towards Equality: Report Of The Committee On The Status Of Women In India* (New Delhi: Government of India Department of Social Welfare, 1974), p. 359.

7. Vina Mazumdar, "Women's Studies and the Women's Movement in India," *Women's Studies Quarterly*, 22:3–4 (Fall-Winter 1994), pp. 42–54.

8. For a detailed discussion of Women's Studies in India, see the "Special Section on Women's Studies in India: Crisis or Renewal?" in the *Indian Journal of Gender Studies*, 9:2 (Jul-Dec, 2002), pp. 203–62, and Neera Desai, Vina Mazumdar, and Kamalini Bhansali, "From women's education to women's studies: The long struggle for legitimacy," in *Narratives From the Women's Studies Family*, eds. Devaki Jain and Pam Rajput, (New Delhi: Sage Publications, 2003), pp. 44–77.

9. Kumud Sharma, "Women's Studies and Higher Education: the Troubled Journey," *Indian Journal of Gender Studies*, p. 209.

10. Sharma, p. 213.

11. Rekha Pappu, "Constituting a Field: Women's Studies in Higher Education," *Indian Journal of Gender Studies*, pp. 221–34.

12. Tanika Sarkar, Plenary Session: "Gendering Historiography," Tenth Berkshire Conference on the History of Women (Jun 7, 1996).

13. Kumkum Sangari and Sudesh Vaid, eds. *Recasting Women, Essays in Colonial History* (New Delhi: Kali for Women, 1989).

14. This essay is also published in Partha Chatterjee, *The Nation and Its Fragments: Colonial and Postcolonial Histories* (Princeton, NJ: Princeton University Press, 1993), p. 130.

15. Tanika Sarkar, *Hindu Wife, Hindu Nation: Gender, Religion and the Prehistory of Indian Nationalism* (London: Hurst and Company, 2001).

16. Sonia Nishat Amin, *The World of Muslim Women in Colonial Bengal* (Leiden: E. J. Brill, 1996); "Rokeya's Padmarag: Utopian Alternative to the Patriarchal Family?" *Dhaka University Studies*, 55: 1 (Jun, 1998), and "Childhood and Role Models in the Andar Mahal," in *Embodied Violence*, eds. Kumari Jayawardena and Malathi De Alwis

(London: Zed Press, 1996). Professor Amin is currently working on a project titled: "Recreating the Victorian Home: Annette Akroyd and Henry Beveridge in Bengal."

17. Swapna Banerjee, *Men, Women, and Domestics: Articulating Middle-Class Identity in Colonial Calcutta* (New Delhi: Oxford University Press, 2004) and "Exploring the World of Domestic Manuals: Bengali Middle-Class Women and Servants in Colonial Calcutta" in *Sagar, South Asia Graduate Research Journal*, 3:1 (Spring 1996). Dr. Banerjee's current research is titled: "Uncovering the Family Story: Children and Childhood in Colonial Bengal."

18. See Judith E. Walsh, *Domesticity in Colonial India: What Women Learned When Men Gave Them Advice* (Lanham: Rowman and Littlefield, 2004).

19. Gayatri Chakravorty Spivak, "Can the Subaltern Speak?" *Marxism and the Interpretation of Culture*, eds. Cary Nelson and Lawrence Grossberg (Urbana: University of Illinois Press, 1988), pp. 271–313, 295.

20. Kamala Visweswaran, "Small Speeches, Subaltern Gender: Nationalist Ideology and Historiography," *Subaltern Studies 9*, eds. Shahid Amin and Dipesh Chakraborty (Delhi: Oxford University Press, 1996), p. 84.

21. Ibid., p. 124.

22. I do not mean to dismiss Subaltern scholarship on gender, I only wish the Collective had produced more articles like Ranajit Guha's "Chandra's Death," *Subaltern Studies 5* (Delhi: Oxford University Press, 1987). All the articles in *Subaltern Studies 11, Community, Gender and Violence*, eds. Partha Chatterjee and Pradeep Jeganathan (NY: Columbia University Press, 2000), refer to gender but not to the subaltern woman.

23. Susie Tharu and K. Lalita, eds. *Women Writing in India, I: 600 B.C. to the Early 20th Century*, 2 Vols. (Delhi: Oxford University Press, 1991, 1993).

24. Shudha Mazumdar, *Memoirs of an Indian Woman,* ed. Geraldine Forbes (Armonk, NY: M.E. Sharpe, 1989); Manmohini Zutshi Sahgal, *An Indian Freedom Fighter Recalls Her Life,* ed. Geraldine Forbes (Armonk, NY: M.E. Sharpe, 1994); *The memoirs of Dr. Haimabati Sen: from child widow to lady doctor,* translated by Tapan Raychaudhuri, edited by Geraldine Forbes and Tapan

Raychaudhuri, introduced by Geraldine Forbes (New Delhi: Roli Books Ltd., 2000).

25. Tanika Sarkar, *Words to Win. The Making of Amar Jiban: A Modern Autobiography* (New Delhi: Kali for Women, 1999).

26. *Binodini Dasi: My Story and My Life As An Actress*, edited and translated by Rimli Bhattacharya (New Delhi: Kali for Women, 1998).

27. Ritu Menon and Kamla Bhasin, "Recovery, Rupture, Resistance: Indian State and Abduction of Women During Partition," *Economic and Political Weekly [EPW]* 28:17 (Apr 24 ,1993), ws2.

28. Urvashi Butalia, *The Other Side of Silence: Voices from the Partition of India* (Delhi: Penguin, 1998). See also, Ritu Menon and Kamla Bhasin, *Borders and Boundaries: Women in India's Partition* (Delhi: Kali for Women, 1998).

29. Butalia, 351.

30. Kanchana Natarajan, "Interfeminine Bonding: Reading Carroll Smith-Rosenberg from a Southern Indian Perspective," *Journal of Women's History* 12: 3 (Autumn, 2000), pp. 13–22

31. Mrinalini Sinha, "Giving Masculinity a History," *Gender and History* 11: 3 (Nov, 1999), pp. 445–60.

32. Antoinette M. Burton. *At the Heart of the Empire: Indians and the Colonial Encounter in Late-Victorian Britain* (Berkeley: University of California Press, 1998).

33. Antoinette Burton. *Dwelling in the Archive: Women Writing House, Home, and History in Late Colonial India* (New York: Oxford University Press, 2002).

34. Burton, *Dwelling in the Archive*, p. 5.

35. Paola Bacchetta, *The Nation and the RSS: gendered discourse, gendered action* (New Delhi: Kali for Women), forthcoming.

36. Flavia Agnes, "Redefining the Agenda of the Women's Movement within a Secular Framework," in Tanika Sarkar and Urvashi Butalia, eds. *Women and Right-Wing Movements: Indian Experiences* (London: Zed Books, 1995), p. 151.

37. Agnes, p. 148.

38. Amrita Basu, "Women's Activism and the Vicissitudes of Hindu Nationalism," *Journal of Women's History*, 10: 4 (Winter, 1999), pp. 104–24.

39. For example, see Tanika Sarkar, "Aspects of Contemporary Hindutva

Theology: The Voice of Sadhvi Ritambhara," in Sarkar, *Hindu Wife, Hindu Nation*, pp. 268–90.

40. Amitabh Ghosh, "In The Reign Of The Headless Horse," *Outlook Magazine* (May 13, 2002).

41. Tanika Sarkar, "Semiotics of Terror: Muslim Children and Women in Hindu Rashtra," *Economic and Political Weekly*, 37: 28 (Jul 13-19 2002), pp. 2875.

42. Refresher Course in Women's Studies, Nov, 1998. From Jadavpur Women's Studies program.

43. The other titles are *Feminist Expressions in Gujarati Short Stories*; *Women in History and the History of Women*; *Issues of Women's Health*; *Women and Education: Development and Challenges*; *Women's Images as Reflected in the Media*; *Landmark Legal Judgments: Theory and Praxis*; *Violence Against Women: Cruel Reality*; and *Women and Economic Participation: Theoretical Analysis*. All volumes except the last have now been published.

44. Interview with Usha Thakkar, Mumbai, Jun 25, 2001.

45. Azra Asghar Ali, *The Emergence of Feminism Among Indian Muslim Women, 1920–1947* (Delhi: Oxford University Press, 2000).

46. Sonia Nishat Amin, *The World of Muslim Women*; Gail Minault, *Secluded Scholars: Women's Education and Muslim Social Reform in Colonial India* (Delhi: Oxford University Press, 1999).

47. Ellison Banks Findly, *Nur Jahan: Empress of Mughal India* (New York: Oxford University Press, 1993); Shaharyar M. Khan, *The Begums of Bhopal: A Dynasty of Women Rulers in Raj India* (London: I.B. Tauris Publishers, 2000); Claudia Preckel, *Begums of Bhopal* (New Delhi: Roli, 2000).

48. Barbara Daly Metcalf, *Perfecting Women: Maulana Ashraf Ali Thanawi's Bihishti Zewar* (Berkeley: University of California Press, 1992).

49. *Hali's Musaddas. A story in verse of the Ebb and tide of Islam*, trans. from the Urdu by Syeda Saiyidain Hameed (New Delhi: Harper Collins, 2003).

50. Siobhan Lambert-Hurley, "Contesting Seclusion: The Political Emergence of Muslim Women in Bhopal, 1901–1930" Ph.D. Dissertation (University of London, 1998).

51. Bilkis Rahman is a Ph.D. candidate in history at Dhaka University.

52. For example, see Uma Chakravarty, "Reconceptualising Gender: Phule, Brahmanism and Brahminical Patriarchy," in *Women in Indian*

History: Social, Economic, Political and Cultural Perspectives, ed. Kiran
Pawar. (Patiala and New Delhi: Vision and Venture, 1996).

53. Anupama Rao, Gender and Caste: Contemporary Issues in Indian
Feminism (New Delhi: Kali for Women, 2003).

54. The Silken Swing: The Cultural Universe of Dalit Women, eds. Fernando
Franco, Jyotsna Macwan, Suguna Ramanthan (Calcutta: Stree, 2000).

55. Srimati Basu, She Comes to Take Her Rights: Indian Women, Property,
and Propriety (Albany: State University of New York, 1999); and Veena
Talwar Oldenburg, Dowry Murder: the Imperial Origins of a Cultural
Crime (New York: Oxford University Press, 2002).

56. See Anshu Malhotra's Gender, Caste, and Religious Identities: Restructuring
Class in Colonial Punjab (Delhi: Oxford University Press, 2002),
and articles: "Of Dais and Midwives: 'Middle-class' Interventions
in the Management of Women's Reproductive Health-A Study
from Colonial Punjab," Indian Journal of Gender Studies. 10:2 (May-
Aug, 2003), pp. 229–60, and "The Body as a Metaphor for the Nation:
Caste, Masculinity, and Femininity in the Satyarth Prakash of Swami
Dayananda Sarasvat," in Rhetoric and Reality: Gender and the Colonial
Experience in South Asia, eds. Avril Powell and Siobhan Lambert-
Hurley (forthcoming).

57. Padma Anagol, Feminism, the Politics of Gender and Social Reform in
India, 1850–1920 (Ashgate: Burlington, forthcoming), and "Indian
Christian women and indigenous feminism, c.1850–c.1920," in
Gender and Imperialism, ed. Clare Midgley (Manchester: Manchester
University Press, 1998).

58. Shefali Chandra, "The Social Life of English. Language and Gender
in Western India 1850–1940," Ph.D. Dissertation (University of
Pennsylvania, 2003).

59. Three papers that speak on this topic were presented as a panel:
"Women and Gender in Modern India: Historians, Sources, and
Historiography," by Barbara Ramusack, Sanjam Ahluwalia, and
Geraldine Forbes, at the Annual Conference of the Association of
Asian Studies (2000). These were published, with comments by
Antoinette Burton, in a special issue of the Journal of Women's History
14:4 (Winter, 2003).

60. SPARROW Annual Report, Apr 1, 1997 to Mar 31, 1998, 3.

61. SPARROW Annual Report, 9. At present this series includes the

following titles all published by SPARROW in Mumbai: *Sakhubai, Talking in the Transplanting Season* (about an agricultural laborer); *Neela, Colours of Tradition* (artist); *Damayanti, Menaka's Daughter* (Kathak dancer); *Sushama, Vhay, mee Savitribai* (actor, activist); *Pramila, Esther Victoria Abraham* (film star); *Jameela Nishat, A Poem Slumbers in My Heart* (poet); *Kanaka, Stone and Gold* (sculptor); *The World as My Laboratory: Shahtoo Gurnani's Tryst with Science* (scientist); *Speaking from the Gut: Memoirs of Communal Riots* (communal riots); *Maya, Vismayah* (dancer); *Amhihi Itihas Ghadawala, Urmila Pawar and the Making of History* (Dalit writer); *Standing on Her Own Two Feet: Kala Shahani* (Gandhian), Roshan G. Shahani, *Allan: Her Infinite Variety* (a Parsi woman's memoir of her mother), and Veena Poonacha, *From the Land of a Thousand Hills* (about her mother, grandmother and great grandmother from Coorg).

62. The workshop on Communalism, Violence and Women, in 1994, was followed by a workshop on Peace and Communal Harmony in 1999 that featured women remembering different communal riots. The oral history narratives from this workshop were published as *Speaking from the Gut* (Mumbai: SPARROW, 1999).

63. Indrani Chatterjee, commentator on panel "The Uses of History in Contemporary South Asia," South Asian Studies (Madison, 2001) raised these questions in her comments.

64. Maitreyi Krishnaraj, "Challenges before Women's Movement in a Changing Context," *Economic and Political Weekly*, 50: 43 (Oct 25, 2003), p. 4536. Krishnaraj's article is one of a series in the Oct 25, 2003 issue of *EPW*. The other two publications I am referring to are the "Special Section on Women's Studies in India: Crisis or Renewal?" in the *Indian Journal of Gender Studies*, and *Narratives From the Women's Studies Family*, eds. Devaki Jain and Pam Rajput, (New Delhi: Sage Publications, 2003).

65. Sharma, p. 217

66. Krishnaraj, p. 4537.

67. Gayatri Spivak, "Discussion: An Afterword on the New Subaltern," *Subaltern Studies 11*, p. 317.

Index